SUMMER MATH WORKBOOK

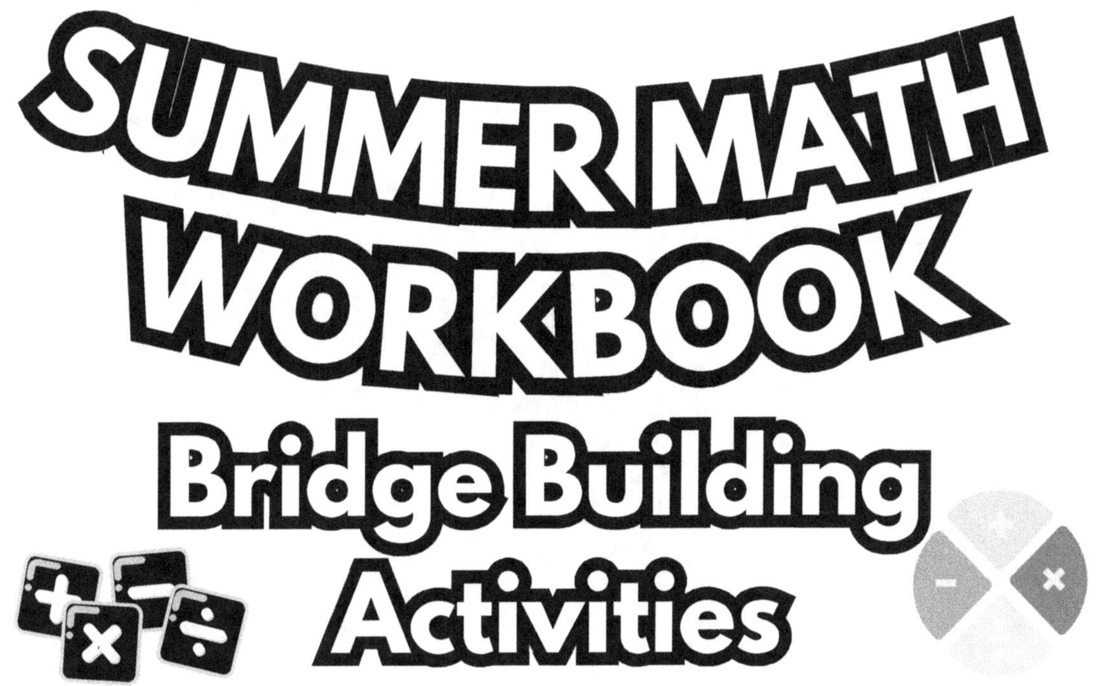

Introduction

As parents and educators, we understand the pivotal role that mathematics plays in shaping a child's academic journey and future success. Yet, the path to mathematical proficiency can often seem daunting, filled with challenges and complexities. That's where the transformative power of Summer Bridge Building Activities books comes into play, illuminating the way forward with clarity, precision, and purpose.

Summer vacation is a time for rest and relaxation, but it also presents the risk of the "summer slide," where students lose some of the academic gains they made during the school year. Summer Bridge Building Activities books are specifically designed to tackle this challenge, ensuring that your child stays academically engaged and prepared for the upcoming school year. These books provide a seamless bridge from one grade to the next, reinforcing essential skills and introducing new concepts that will give your child a head start.

Imagine your child eagerly diving into the pages of a Summer Bridge Building Activities book, greeted by clear, engaging content that demystifies complex mathematical concepts. With each turn of the pages, they embark on a journey of discovery, encountering thoughtfully curated practice questions that reinforce learning and sharpen problem-solving skills. As they unveil the answers to those questions, a sense of accomplishment blossoms within them — a tangible reward for their hard work and dedication.

Summer Bridge Building Activities books transcend traditional educational tools; they are meticulously crafted to build a deep and enduring understanding of mathematics. These books follow a sequential and logical progression, starting from fundamental principles and advancing to sophisticated problem-solving strategies. Each chapter is designed to build on the previous one, ensuring a solid and comprehensive foundation for future learning.

Parents, we yearn for nothing more than to see our children thrive academically and personally. We want to witness the spark of inspiration ignited within them as they overcome academic challenges with confidence and poise. Summer Bridge Building Activities books serve as indispensable partners in this noble endeavor, offering not just practice questions but the keys to unlocking a world of academic and personal opportunities.

Visualize the pride on your child's face as they master a challenging math concept, the joy they experience when their efforts yield results, and the confidence they gain with each success. These pages are designed to make learning math a positive, enriching, and deeply rewarding experience that will benefit them throughout their academic journey and beyond.

For educators, Summer Bridge Building Activities books are invaluable allies in the quest to cultivate mathematical proficiency in the classroom. Accompanied by comprehensive guides and readily available answers, instructors can focus on mentoring and nurturing their students, secure in the knowledge that these books provide a robust framework for effective learning.

Within the pages of Summer Bridge Building Activities books lies not just the promise of academic excellence, but the seeds of a brighter future. By integrating these resources into your child's summer routine, you are bestowing upon them the gifts of confidence, curiosity, and a lifelong love of learning.

Invest in your child's future today with Summer Bridge Building Activities books — because every great journey begins with a single step, and this step can change everything. Keep the momentum of learning alive over the summer, and watch your child soar to new academic heights.

Contents

Grade
1 → 2
SUMMER MATH
WORKBOOK
Bridge Building
Activities
Number Sense
Addition and Subtraction
Place Value

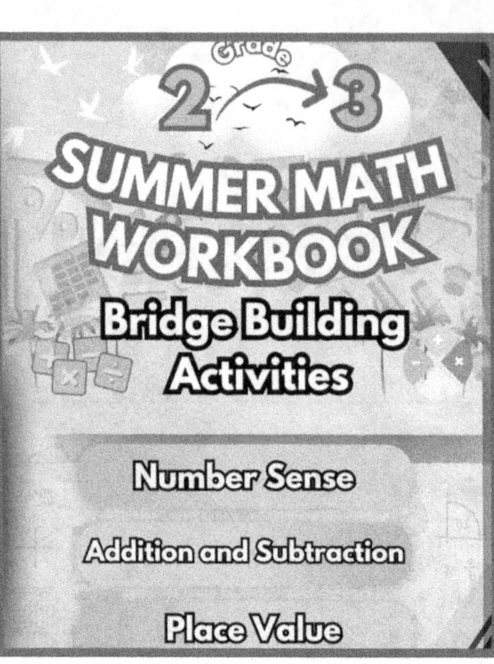

Grade
2 → 3
SUMMER MATH
WORKBOOK
Bridge Building
Activities
Number Sense
Addition and Subtraction
Place Value

Grade
3 → 4
SUMMER MATH
WORKBOOK
Bridge Building
Activities
Number Sense
Addition and Subtraction
Place Value

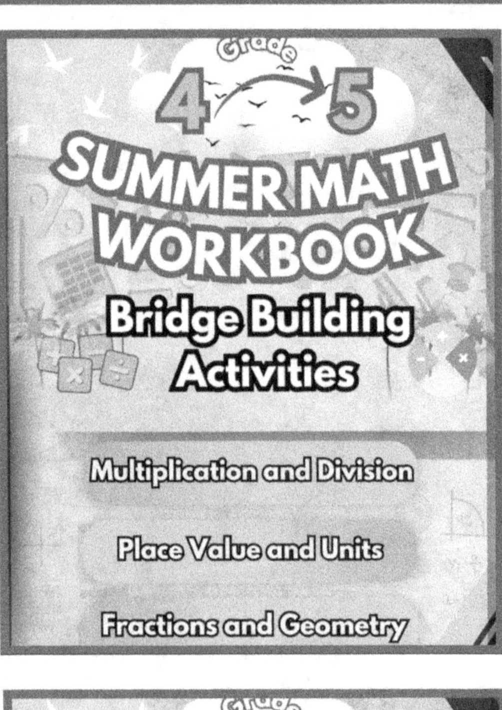

Grade
4 → 5
SUMMER MATH
WORKBOOK
Bridge Building
Activities
Multiplication and Division
Place Value and Units
Fractions and Geometry

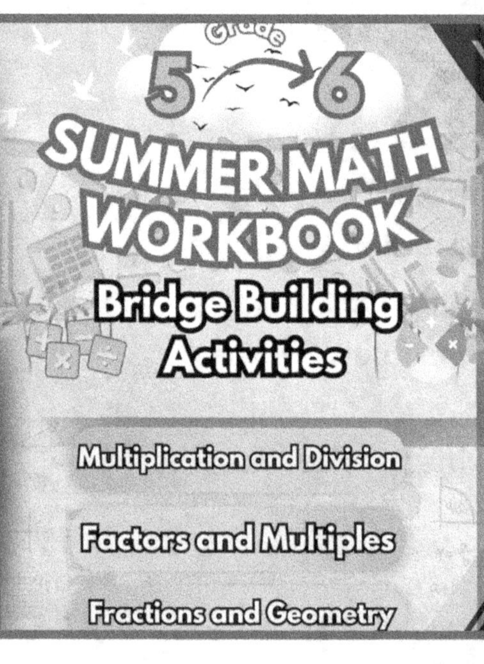

Grade
5 → 6
SUMMER MATH
WORKBOOK
Bridge Building
Activities
Multiplication and Division
Factors and Multiples
Fractions and Geometry

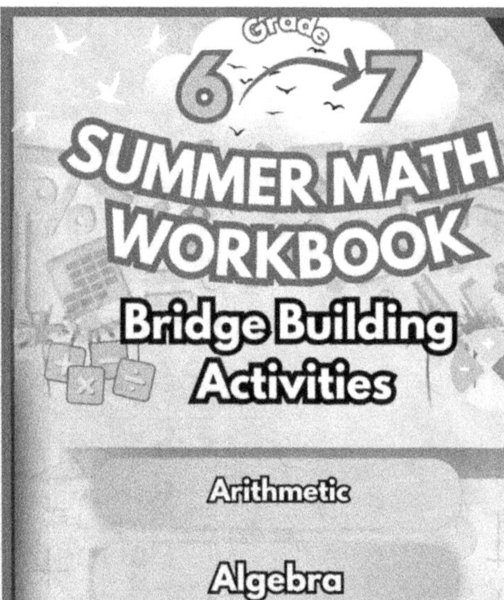

Grade
6 → 7
SUMMER MATH
WORKBOOK
Bridge Building
Activities
Arithmetic
Algebra
Geometry and Statistics

Grade
7 → 8
SUMMER MATH
WORKBOOK
Bridge Building
Activities
Ratio and Percentage
Algebra and Cartesian Plane
Geometry and Statistics

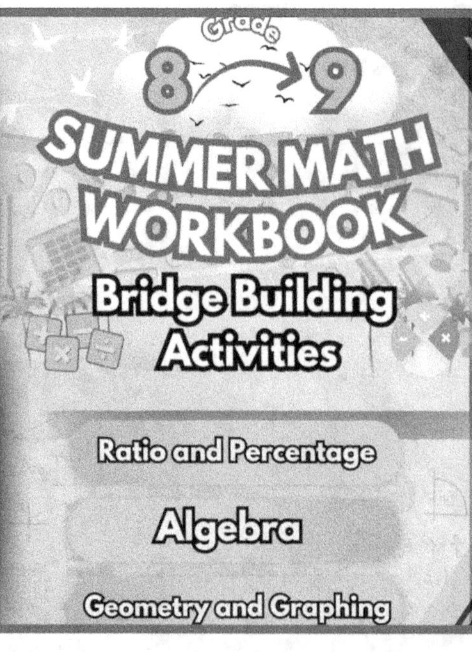

Grade
8 → 9
SUMMER MATH
WORKBOOK
Bridge Building
Activities
Ratio and Percentage
Algebra
Geometry and Graphing

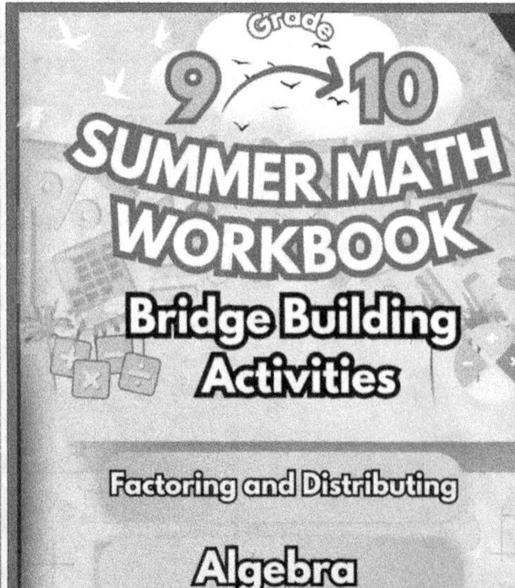

Grade
9 → 10
SUMMER MATH
WORKBOOK
Bridge Building
Activities
Factoring and Distributing
Algebra
Geometry and Graphing

Equations and Expressions

Simplifying expressions

It involves combining like terms and performing operations to make the expression easier to understand and work with.

Let's simplify the expression:

$$2x - 2x + 8 + 4$$

- **Combine like terms:** First, we look for terms with the same variable and exponent. In this expression, $2x$ and $-2x$ are like terms, so they can be combined:

$$2x - 2x = 0$$

- **Substitute the simplified terms:** After combining the like terms, the expression becomes:

$$0 + 8 + 4$$

- **Combine the remaining terms:** Now, we add the constants together:

$$8 + 4 = 12$$

Solving Equations

Evaluating expressions involves substituting given values for variables in an expression and then performing the indicated operations to find the result.

For example: Let's evaluate $4x - 10$, when $x = 3$:

Step 1: Substitute the given value for the variable:

Replace every occurrence of x in the expression 4x – 10 with the given value, which is 3:

$$= 4(3) - 10$$

Step 2: Perform the operations:

Perform the indicated operations according to the order of operations (PEMDAS - Parentheses, Exponents, Multiplication and Division, Addition and Subtraction):

$$= 4 \times 3 - 10$$

Step 3: Simplify:

Calculate the result:

$$12 - 10 = 2$$

Solving Equations (One Side)

Solving one-step equations involves performing a single operation to isolate the variable and find its value.

Let's solve an equation step by step: **16 + x = 31**

1. **Identify the Goal**:

    The goal is to isolate the variable x on one side of the equation.

2. **Simplify the Equation**: Combine like terms on both sides of the equation, if necessary.

    The equation is already simplified.

3. **Undo Addition or Subtraction**: If there's addition or subtraction involving the variable, undo it by performing the opposite operation on both sides of the equation.

Since x is being added to 16, we'll undo this operation by subtracting 16 from both sides of the equation:

$$16 + x - 16 = 31 - 16$$

4. **Isolate the Variable**: Ensure that the variable is alone on one side of the equation.

$$x = 15$$

5. **Check Your Solution**: Substitute the value of x back into the original equation to verify that it satisfies the equation.

$$16 + 15 = 31$$

$$31 = 31$$

The equation is balanced.

Equations (Two Sides)

A two-sided equation is an equation where both sides have expressions with variables and constants. The goal when solving a two-sided equation is to find the value of the variable that makes both sides equal.

For example: Let's solve an equation:

$$9 + 8x + 8 = 64 + x + 2$$

- **Combine Like Terms:** Simplify each side of the equation by combining like terms (terms with the same variable or constants).

$$9 + 8x + 8 = 64 + x + 2$$

$$17 + 8x = 66 + x$$

- **Isolate the Variable:** Use inverse operations to isolate the variable on one side of the equation.

$$\text{subtract } x \text{ from both sides:}$$

$$17 + 8x - x = 66 + x - x$$

$$17 + 7x = 66$$

$$\text{subtracting } 17 \text{ from both sides:}$$

$$17 - 17 + 7x = 66 - 17$$

$$7x = 49$$

$$\text{divide both sides by 7:}$$

$$\frac{7x}{7} = \frac{49}{7} = x = 7$$

- **Check Solution:** Once you find the solution, substitute it back into the original equation to ensure it makes the equation true.

$$\text{Substitute } x = 7 \text{ back into the original equation:}$$

$$9 + 8(7) + 8 = 64 + 7 + 2$$

$$9 + 56 + 8 = 64 + 7 + 2$$

$$73 = 73$$

Verbal Algebra Expressions

Verbal algebra involves translating word problems or verbal statements into algebraic expressions or equations.

For example: The product of the two numbers is 91. One number is six less than the other. What are the numbers?

We're given a verbal description of a problem, and we need to represent it using algebraic symbols and equations.

Let's break down the given problem into algebraic expressions:

- Given that the product of the two numbers is 91, we can write the equation: $xy = 91$
- Also, given that one number is six less than the other, we can write another equation: $x = y - 6$

Now, we can use algebraic techniques to solve the system of equations to find the values of x and y, which represent the two numbers.

$$x(x - 6) = 91$$

1. **Solve the equation:**

   - Expand the equation:

   $$x^2 - 6x = 91$$

   - Rearrange the equation into standard quadratic form:

   $$x^2 - 6x - 91 = 0$$

   - Factor the quadratic equation:

   $$(x - 13)(x + 7) = 0$$

2. **Find the solutions for x:**

   - From the factored form, we have two possible values for x:

   $$x = 13 \text{ or } x = -7$$

3. **Check the validity of the solutions:**

- Since one number is six less than the other, we discard the negative solution.

- Therefore, the solution is $x = 13$.

4. **Find the other number:**

- Substitute $x = 13$ into the expression for the other number:

Other number $= x - 6 = 13 - 6 = 7$

So, the two numbers are 13 and 7.

Linear Equation

Understanding Linear Functions

A linear equation is an algebraic equation that represents a straight line when graphed on a coordinate plane. It consists of variables raised to the power of 1 (i.e., no exponents higher than 1) and constant coefficients.

The general form of a linear equation in one variable x is:

$$ax + b = 0$$

Where a and b are constants, and x is the variable.

Let's solve the linear equation:

$$-2x + 9 = 5$$

- **Isolate the variable term:** We want to isolate the term containing x on one side of the equation. To do this, we'll move the constant term to the other side. Subtract 9 from both sides:

$$-2x + 9 - 9 = 5 - 9$$

$$-2x = -4$$

- **Divide by the coefficient of the variable:** To solve for x, divide both sides by the coefficient of x, which is -2:

$$\frac{-2x}{-2} = \frac{-4}{-2}$$

$$x = 2$$

<u>**Slop from Two Points**</u>

The slope between two points on a Cartesian coordinate system is a measure of the steepness of the line connecting those points. It's calculated by finding the change in the y-coordinates divided by the change in the x-coordinates.

- The coordinates of the first point as $(x1 , y1) = (2, -30)$.

- The coordinates of the second point as $(x2 , y2) = (-5, 40)$.

The formula to calculate the slope (m) between two points:

$$\frac{y2 - y1}{x2 - x1}$$

$$= \frac{40 - (-30)}{-5 - 2} = \frac{70}{-7}$$

Slope = -10

System of Equations

A system of equations is a collection of two or more equations involving the same set of variables. The solution to a system of equations is the set of values for the variables that satisfy all the equations simultaneously.

Solving by Elimination:

To solve a system of equations by elimination, we manipulate the equations to eliminate one of the variables.

Given the system:

$$4x + 5y = 6$$

$$10x + 6y = 8$$

Step 1: Multiply each equation by a constant such that the coefficients of one of the variables become equal or multiples of each other.

Let's try to eliminate the variable x.

- Multiply the first equation by 5 and the second equation by -2:

$$20x + 25y = 30$$

$$-20x - 12y = -16$$

Step 2: Add the two equations together to eliminate the variable x:

$$(20x - 20x) + (25y - 12y) = 30 - 16$$

$$13y = 14$$

Step 3: Solve for *y*:

$$y = \frac{14}{13} = 1.077$$

Step 4: Substitute the value of y into one of the original equations to solve for x. Let's use the first equation:

$$4x + 5\left(\frac{14}{13}\right) = 6$$

$$4x + \frac{70}{13} = 6$$

$$4x = 6 - \frac{70}{13}$$

$$4x = \frac{78 - 70}{13}$$

$$4x = \frac{8}{13}$$

$$x = \frac{2}{13} = 0.154$$

the solution to the system of equations is x = 0.154 and y = 1.077.

<u>Quadratic Equations</u>

A quadratic equation is a polynomial equation of the second degree, meaning it can be written in the form:

$$ax^2 + bx + c = 0$$

where a, b, and c are constants, and x is the variable being solved for. The solutions to a quadratic equation are the values of x that make the equation true.

Now, let's solve the quadratic equation **$11x^2 - 1 = 0$** and understand it step by step using quadratic formula.

1. **Identify the coefficients:**

   In the equation $11x^2 - 1 = 0$,

   $$a=11, b=0, \text{ and } c=-1.$$

2. **Apply the quadratic formula:**

   The quadratic formula states that for an equation $ax^2 + bx + c = 0$, the solutions for x are given by:

   $$x = \frac{-b \pm \sqrt{b^2 - 4ac}}{2a}$$

   Plugging in the values a=11, b=0, and c=−1 into the quadratic formula, we get:

   $$x = \frac{-0 \pm \sqrt{0 - 4(11)(-1)}}{2(11)}$$

3. **Simplify inside the square root:**

$$0^2 - 4(11)\,(-1) = 0 - (-44) = 44$$

4. **Plug in the simplified values:**

$$x = \frac{\pm\sqrt{44}}{22}$$

5. **Simplify the square root:**

Since 44 is not a perfect square, we can write it as $\sqrt[2]{11}$

$$x = \frac{\pm\sqrt[2]{11}}{22}$$

6. **Simplify further if possible:**

We can simplify $\sqrt[2]{11}$ to $\sqrt{11}$ by canceling out the common factor:

$$x = \frac{\pm\sqrt{11}}{11}$$

7. **Final solution:**

So, the solutions to the equation are:

$$x = \frac{\sqrt{11}}{11} \text{ and } x = \frac{-\sqrt{11}}{11}$$

$$\text{or}$$

$$(x = 0.302, \text{ and } x = -0.302)$$

These are the roots of the quadratic equation. They represent the points where the graph of the quadratic equation intersects the x-axis.

Let's solve another equation:

$$-4p^2 + 6p - 6 = 0$$

$$p = \frac{-b \pm \sqrt{b^2 - 4ac}}{2a}$$

where $a = -4$, $b = 6$, and $c = -6$.

Let's plug these values into the quadratic formula:

$$p = \frac{-6 \pm \sqrt{6^2 - 4(-4)(-6)}}{2(-4)}$$

First, let's simplify inside the square root:

$$6^2 - 4\,(-4)\,(-6)$$

$$= 36 - 96 = -60$$

So, we have:

$$p = \frac{-6 \pm \sqrt{-60}}{-8}$$

We can simplify the square root of −60 by factoring out −1:

$$\sqrt{-60}$$

$$= \sqrt{-1 \times 60}$$

$$= \sqrt{-1} \times \sqrt{60}$$

$$= i\sqrt{60}$$

So, we have:

$$p = \frac{-6 \pm i\sqrt{60}}{-8}$$

Simplify:

$$\sqrt{60} \text{ to } \sqrt{4 \times 15} = 2\sqrt{15}$$

$$p = \frac{-6 \pm i \times 2\sqrt{15}}{-8}$$

Now, divide both the numerator and denominator by −2 to simplify:

$$p = \frac{3 \pm i\sqrt{15}}{4}$$

So, the solutions to the equation are:

$$p = \frac{3 + i\sqrt{15}}{4} \text{ and } p = \frac{3 - i\sqrt{15}}{4}$$

This equation **-4p² + 6p - 6 = 0** has no real solutions.

When a quadratic equation has no real solutions, it means that the solutions are not real numbers, but rather complex numbers. In this case, the solutions involve the imaginary unit i because the discriminant (b^2-4ac) is negative, which results in taking the square root of a negative number when applying the quadratic formula.

In mathematics, such equations are said to have "no real roots" or "no real solutions." They are also sometimes referred to as having "complex roots" or "complex solutions." Complex numbers include a real part and an imaginary part, and they are often written in the form $a + bi$, where a and b are real numbers and i is the imaginary unit, defined as $i = \sqrt{-1}$.

Let's solve another equation:

$$12x^2 + 6x - 2 = 0$$

$$x = \frac{-b \pm \sqrt{b^2 - 4ac}}{2a}$$

where $a = 12$, $b = 6$, and $c = -2$.

Let's plug these values into the quadratic formula:

$$x = \frac{-6 \pm \sqrt{6^2 - 4(12)(-2)}}{2(12)}$$

First, let's simplify inside the square root:

$$6^2 - 4(12)(-2)$$

$$= 36 - (-96)$$

$$= 36 + 96$$

$$= 132$$

So, we have:

$$x = \frac{-6 \pm \sqrt{132}}{24}$$

Now, let's simplify the square root of 132:

$$x = \frac{-6 \pm \sqrt{4 \times 33}}{24}$$

$$x = \frac{-6 \pm 2\sqrt{33}}{24}$$

$$x = \frac{-6 \pm \sqrt{33}}{12}$$

So, the solutions to the equation are:

$$x = \frac{-6 + \sqrt{33}}{12} \text{ and } x = \frac{-6 - \sqrt{33}}{12}$$

or (x = 0.229, and x = -0.729)

Let's solve a Quadratic Equation where the right side is a number instead of 0.

$$-8n^2 + 6n + 30 = 7$$

To solve the equation, we first need to bring all terms to one side to set the equation equal to zero:

$$-8n^2 + 6n + 30 - 7 = 0$$

Simplify:

$$-8n^2 + 6n + 23 = 0$$

Now, to solve for n, we can use the quadratic formula:

$$n = \frac{-b \pm \sqrt{b^2 - 4ac}}{2a}$$

where $a = -8$, $b = 6$, and $c = 23$.

Plugging these values into the formula, we get:

$$n = \frac{-6 \pm \sqrt{6^2 - 4(-8)(23)}}{2(-8)}$$

$$n = \frac{-6 \pm \sqrt{36 + 736}}{-16}$$

$$n = \frac{-6 \pm \sqrt{772}}{-16}$$

Now, let's simplify the square root of 772. We can factor out 4:

$$\sqrt{772} = \sqrt{4 \times 193} = 2\sqrt{193}$$

So, our equation becomes:

$$n = \frac{-6 \pm 2\sqrt{193}}{-8}$$

So, the solutions to the equation are:

$$n = \frac{-3 + \sqrt{193}}{-8} \quad \text{and} \quad n = \frac{-3 - \sqrt{193}}{-8}$$

or

$$(n = -1.362, \text{ and } n = 2.112)$$

Polynomials

A polynomial is an algebraic expression consisting of one or more terms, where each term is a constant, a variable, or a product of constants and variables raised to whole number exponents.

Examples of polynomials include:

- $(7v^2 + 2v^4) + (8v^2 + 4v^4)$
- $(2v + 4v^2 + 2) - (5v - 4v^4 - 6v^2)$
- $(7x - 5\,y)(2x - 6\,y)$
- $(6x^2 + 4xy + 6\,y^2)(8x^2 + 3xy + 3\,y^2)$
- $\dfrac{2x^3 + 8x^2 + 2x}{2x^2}$

Operations on Polynomials

Addition of Polynomials:

- To add polynomials, simply combine like terms.
- Like terms are terms that have the same variable(s) raised to the same power(s).
- For example, to add $3x^2 + 2x$ and $5x^2 - 7x$, group the like terms: $3x^2 + 5x^2$ and $2x - 7x$, then add each group separately.

Subtraction of Polynomials:

- To subtract polynomials, distribute the negative sign and then add.
- For example, to subtract $x^2 - 2x$ from $4x^2 + 3x$, distribute the negative sign to each term in the second polynomial: $-(x^2 - 2x)$, then add each term separately.

Multiplication of Polynomials:

- To multiply polynomials, use the distributive property and then combine like terms.

- For example, to multiply $(x + 2)(3x - 4)$, distribute each term in the first polynomial to each term in the second polynomial, then combine like terms.

Division of Polynomials:

- Division of polynomials involves dividing one polynomial by another. It can be done using long division or synthetic division.

Let's solve the expression:

$$(7x^2 \cdot 7x) \cdot (x \cdot 2x^2)$$

Step 1: Distribute the Negative Sign:

Distribute the negative sign in the second polynomial:

$$(7x^2 - 7x) - x + 2x^2$$

Step 2: Combine Like Terms:

$$(7x^2 + 2x^2) + (- 7x - x)$$

Step 3: Perform addition and subtraction of coefficients:

$$9x^2 - 8x$$

Let's perform the multiplication of polynomials:

$$(5u + 2v)(8u^2 \cdot uv \cdot 3v^2)$$

We can distribute each term in the first polynomial $(5u+2v)$ to every term in the second polynomial $(8u2 - uv - 3v2)$.

1. **Multiply $5u$ by each term in the second polynomial:**

$$5u \cdot 8u^2 = 40u^3$$
$$5u \cdot (-uv) = -5u^2v$$

$$5u \cdot (-3v^2) = -15uv^2$$

2. Multiply $2v$ by each term in the second polynomial:

$$2v \cdot 8u^2 = 16u^2v$$
$$2v \cdot (-uv) = -2uv^2$$
$$2v \cdot (-3v^2) = -6v^3$$

Combine the like terms:

$$40u^3 - 5u^2v - 15uv^2 + 16u^2v - 2uv^2 - 6v^3$$

Combine the like terms involving u and v:

$$40u^3 + (16u^2v - 5u^2v) + (-15uv^2 - 2uv^2) - 6v^3$$
$$40u^3 + 11u^2v - 17uv^2 - 6v^3$$

<u>Geometry</u>

<u>Area and Perimeter</u>

The area of a shape represents the amount of space it occupies. The perimeter of a shape is the total distance around its outer edge.

Area of Rectangle

For a square, since all four sides are equal, we only need to know the length of one side to find its area. We can calculate the area of a square by multiplying the length of one side by itself (squared). So, if the length of one side of the square is 's', then the area (A) is given by:

$$A = s \times s$$

4 in

4 in

$$A = 4 \times 4$$

$$A = 16$$

Perimeter of Rectangle

For a square, since all four sides are equal, we can find the perimeter by adding up the lengths of all four sides. If 's' represents the length of one side, then the perimeter (P) is given by:

$$P = 4 \times s$$

$$P = 4 \times 4$$

$$P = 16$$

Area of Triangle:

The area of a triangle represents the amount of space enclosed within its three sides. The formula for calculating the area of a triangle depends on the type of triangle. For a general triangle, we use the formula:

$$A = \frac{1}{2} \times \text{base} \times \text{height}$$

Where:

- A represents the area of the triangle.

- The base is the length of any one side of the triangle.

- The height is the perpendicular distance from the base to the opposite vertex.

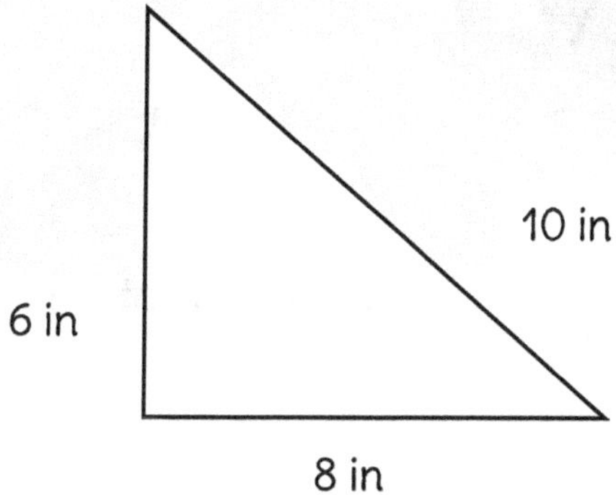

$$A = \frac{1}{2} \times base \times height$$

$$A = \frac{1}{2} \times 6 \times 8$$

$$A = \frac{1}{2} \times 48$$

$$A = 24$$

Perimeter of Triangle:

The perimeter of a triangle is the total length of its three sides. To find the perimeter, we simply add the lengths of all three sides together:

$$P = side1 + side2 + side3$$

$$P = 6 + 8 + 10$$

$$P = 24$$

Equilateral Triangle

An equilateral triangle is a triangle in which all three sides are equal in length. To find the area and perimeter of an equilateral triangle, we can use the following formulas:

- Area (A): $\frac{\sqrt{3}}{4} \times a^2$ where a is the length of one side of the equilateral triangle.
- Perimeter (P): $P = 3a$ where a is the length of one side of the equilateral triangle.

Area of Equilateral Triangle:

$$\text{Area (A): } \frac{\sqrt{3}}{4} \times (6)^2$$

$$\text{Area (A): } \frac{\sqrt{3}}{4} \times 36$$

$$\text{Area (A): } \frac{36\sqrt{3}}{4}$$

$$\text{Area (A): } \frac{36(1.73)}{4}$$

$$\text{Area (A): } \frac{62.35}{4}$$

$$\text{Area (A): } 15.59 \text{ in}^2$$

Perimeter of Equilateral Triangle:

$$P = 3a$$

$$P = 3(6) = 18$$

Isosceles Triangle

An isosceles triangle is a triangle with at least two sides of equal length. The angles opposite the equal sides are also equal.

Area of Isosceles Triangle

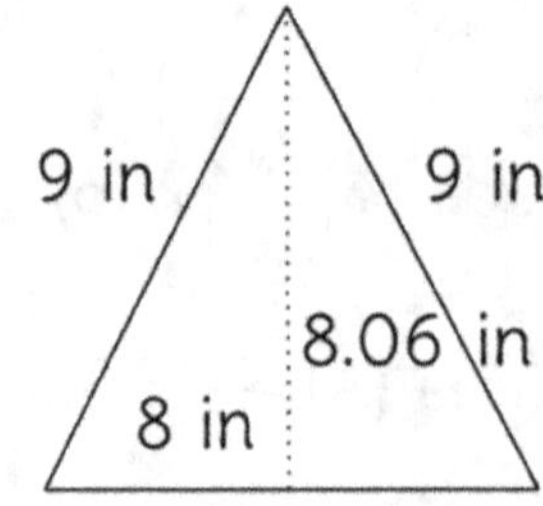

$$A = \frac{1}{2} \times \text{base} \times \text{height}$$

$$A = \frac{1}{2} \times 8 \times 8$$

$$A = \frac{1}{2} \times 64$$

$$A = 32$$

Perimeter of Isosceles Triangle

The perimeter of a triangle is the total length of its three sides. To find the perimeter, we simply add the lengths of all three sides together:

$$P = \text{side1} + \text{side2} + \text{side3}$$

$$P = 9 + 9 + 8$$

$$P = 26$$

Scalene Triangle

A scalene triangle is a triangle with no equal sides and no equal angles. The formula for finding various properties of a scalene triangle is as follows:

Area (A): The area of a scalene triangle can be calculated using Heron's fo rmula, which is given by:

$$A = \sqrt{s(s-a)(s-b)(s-c)}$$

where s is the semi-perimeter of the triangle,

and a, b, and c are the lengths of its three sides.

Perimeter (P): The perimeter of a scalene triangle is the sum of the lengths of its three sides.

$$P = side1 + side2 + side3$$

Let's find the Area and Perimeter of a Scalene Triangle:

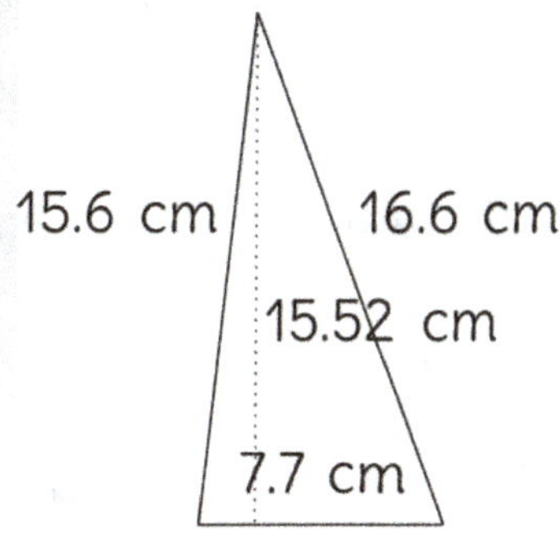

Area (A): First, we calculate the semi-perimeter (s):

$$S = \frac{a+b+c}{2} = \frac{15.6 + 16.6 + 7.7}{2} = \frac{39.8}{2} = 19.9 \text{ cm}$$

Heron's formula to find the area:

$$A = \sqrt{s(s-a)(s-b)(s-c)}$$

$$A = \sqrt{19.9\,(19.9 - 15.6)\,(19.9 - 16.6)\,(19.9 - 7.7)}$$

$$A = \sqrt{19.9 \times 4.3 \times 3.3 \times 12.2}$$

$$A = \sqrt{3445} \approx 59$$

Perimeter (P):

$$P = side1 + side2 + side3$$

$$P = 15.6 + 16.6 + 7.7$$

$$P = 39.8$$

Area and Perimeter of an L-shape

The L-shaped figure typically consists of two rectangles joined together to form an L-shape. To find the area and perimeter of an L-shaped figure, we will need to calculate the areas and perimeters of each rectangle and then combine them.

Area=Area of Rectangle 1 + Area of Rectangle 2

Perimeter=Perimeter of Rectangle 1 + Perimeter of Rectangle 2

Let's find the Area and Perimeter of an L-shape:

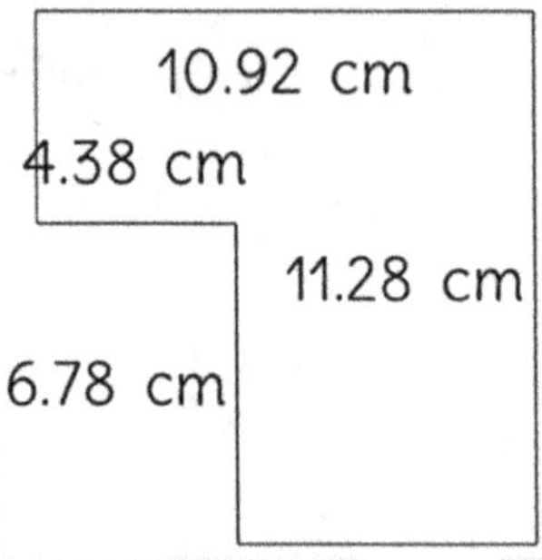

Area of L-Shape

$$Area\ 1 = 4.38 \times 4.5 = 19.7\ cm^2$$

$$Area\ 2 = 11.28 \times 6.54 = 73.7\ cm^2$$

$$Area = 19.7 + 73.7$$

$$\text{Area} = 93.481 \text{ cm}^2$$

Perimeter of L-Shape

$$P = 11.28 + 6.54 + 6.78 + 4.38 + 4.5 + 10.92$$

$$P = 44.4 \text{ cm}$$

Area and Perimeter of U-shape

U-shape is basically composed of three rectangles, we'll need to calculate the area and perimeter of each rectangle separately and then sum them up.

Area of the U-shape:

The total area (A) of the U-shape is the sum of the areas of the three rectangles:

$$A = A1 + A2 + A3$$

Perimeter of the U-shape: The total perimeter (P) of the U-shape is the sum of the perimeters of the three rectangles:

$$P = P1 + P2 + P3$$

Let's find the area and perimeter of the following U-shape:

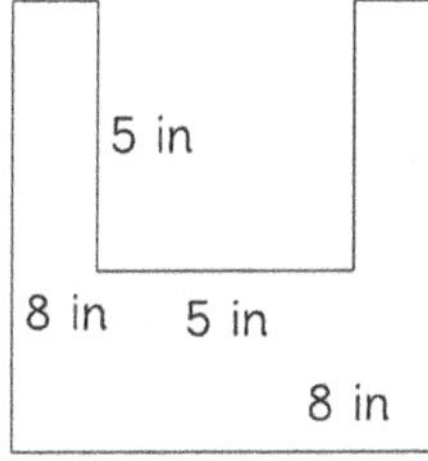

Area:

$$A1 = 8 \times 1.5 = 12 + A2 = 3 \times 5 = 15 + A3 = 8 \times 1.5 = 12$$

$$= 12 + 15 + 12$$

$$= 39 \text{ in}^2$$

Perimeter:

$$2 \times 8 + 2 \times 5 + 2 \times 8$$

$$= 16 + 10 + 16$$

$$= 42$$

Area and Perimeter of T-shape

The T-shape consists of two rectangles joined together to form a T-like structure.

Area of the T-shape:

To find the total area of the T-shape, we need to calculate the areas of both rectangles and then add them together.

$$\text{Area of Rectangle 1} = \text{Length} \times \text{Width}$$

$$\text{Area of Rectangle 2} = \text{Length} \times \text{Width}$$

$$\text{Total Area} = \text{Area of Rectangle 1} + \text{Area of Rectangle 2}$$

The perimeter of the T-shape is the sum of the perimeters of the two rectangles, minus the length of the overlapping side:

$$\text{Perimeter} = 2(l1+w1) + 2(l2+w2) - (w1\text{-}w2)$$

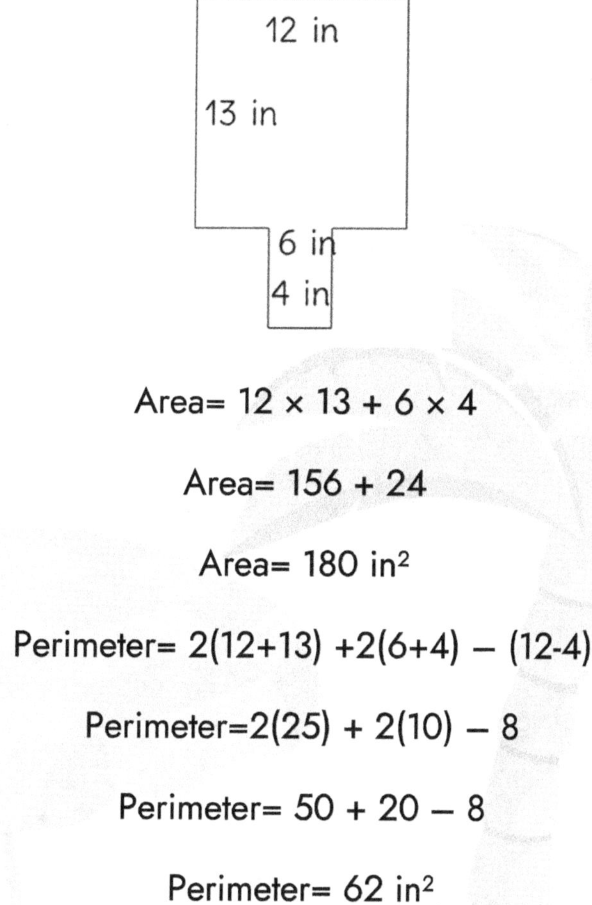

Area= 12 × 13 + 6 × 4

Area= 156 + 24

Area= 180 in²

Perimeter= 2(12+13) +2(6+4) − (12-4)

Perimeter=2(25) + 2(10) − 8

Perimeter= 50 + 20 − 8

Perimeter= 62 in²

<u>Area and Perimeter of Parallelogram</u>

A parallelogram is a four-sided polygon with opposite sides that are parallel and equal in length. To find the area and perimeter of a parallelogram, we use specific formulas based on its dimensions.

For example:

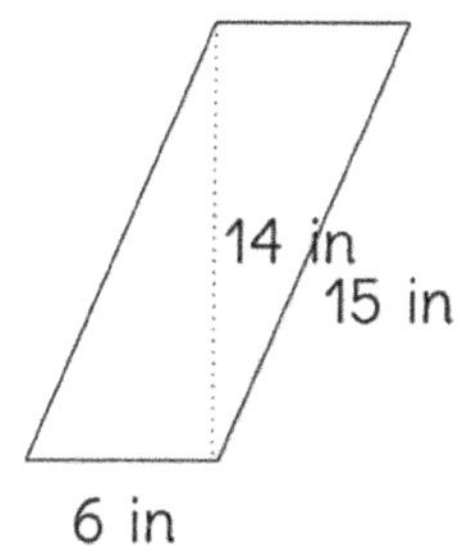

Let's denote:

- The length of one side of the parallelogram as $a = 15$.

- The length of an adjacent side (parallel to a) $b = 6$.

- The height of the parallelogram (perpendicular distance between the two parallel sides) as $h=14$

Area of Parallelogram

$$\text{Area} = \text{Base} \times \text{Height}$$

$$\text{Area} = 6 \times 1\,4$$

$$\text{Area} = 84$$

Perimeter of Parallelogram

$$2(a + b)$$

$$= 2(15+6)$$

$$= 2(21)$$

$$= 42$$

Area and Perimeter of Trapezoids

A trapezoid is a quadrilateral with at least one pair of parallel sides. To find the area and perimeter of a trapezoid, we use specific formulas based on its dimensions.

For example:

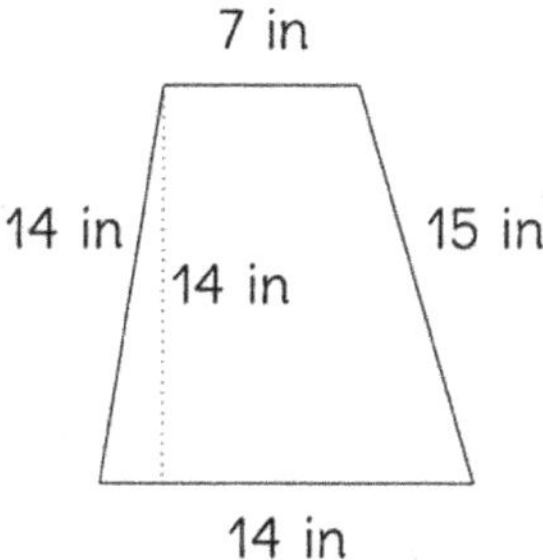

Let's denote:

- The lengths of the parallel sides of the trapezoid as $a = 7$ and $b = 14$.

- The lengths of the non-parallel sides as $c = 14$ and $d = 15$.

- The height of the trapezoid (the perpendicular distance between the parallel sides) as $h=14$.

Area of the Trapezoid:

The area of a trapezoid is given by the formula:

$$\text{Area} = \frac{1}{2} \times \text{Height} \times (\text{Sum of the lengths of the parallel sides})$$

$$\text{Area} = \frac{1}{2} \times h \times (a + b)$$

$$\text{Area} = \frac{1}{2} \times 14 \times (7 + 14)$$

$$\text{Area} = \frac{1}{2} \times 14 \times 21$$

$$\text{Area} = 147 \text{ in}^2$$

Perimeter of the Trapezoid:

$$\text{Perimeter} = 7 + 14 + 14 + 15$$

$$= 50 \text{ in}^2$$

Pythagorean Theorem

The Pythagorean Theorem is a fundamental principle in geometry that relates the lengths of the sides of a right triangle. It states that in any right triangle, the square of the length of the hypotenuse (the side opposite the right angle) is equal to the sum of the squares of the lengths of the other two sides.

$$a2 + b2 = c2$$

Let's use the Pythagorean Theorem to find the length of the hypotenuse (c) when $a=44$ and $b=78$.

$$c^2 = 44^2 + 78^2$$
$$c^2 = 1936 + 6084 \qquad c = \sqrt{8020}$$
$$c^2 = 8020 \qquad c \approx 89.554$$

Volume and surface Area

Volume refers to the amount of space occupied by a three-dimensional object. For shapes like cubes or rectangular prisms, we calculate volume by multiplying their length, width, and height.

To find the volume V of a rectangular prism, we use the formula:

$$Volume \ = \ length \ x \ width \ x \ height$$

Surface Area represents the total area covering all the faces of a three-dimensional object. For shapes like cubes or rectangular prisms, we find the surface area by summing the areas of all its faces.

The formula for surface area SA of a cube or rectangular prism is:

$$Surface\ Area\ =\ 2lw\ +\ 2lh\ +\ 2wh$$

Where: l is the length, w is the width, and h is the height of the object.

For example: Let's find the Volume and Surface Area of following rectangular prisms:

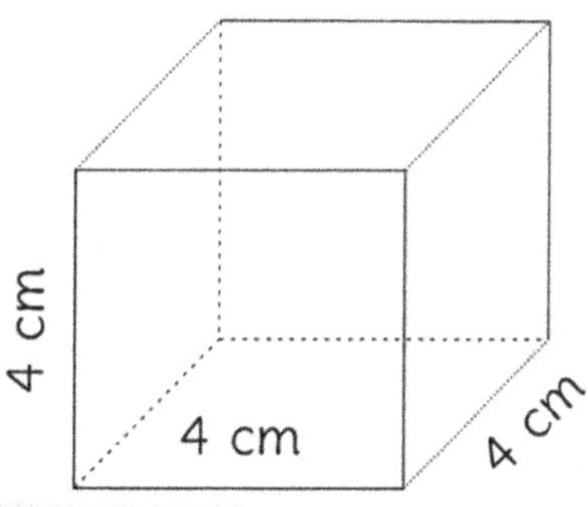

$$Volume\ =\ length\ \times\ width\ \times\ height$$

$$=\ 4 \times 4 \times 4$$

$$=\ 64\ cm^2$$

$$Surface\ Area\ =\ 2lw\ +\ 2lh\ +\ 2wh$$

$$=\ 2(4 \times 4) + 2(4 \times 4) + 2(4 \times 4)$$

$$=\ 32 + 32 + 32$$

$$=\ 96\ cm2$$

Different 3D objects have unique formulas for finding their volume and surface area. Here are some common ones:

1. Cube:

- Volume: $V = s^3$ (where s is the length of one side of the cube)

- Surface area: $SA = 6s^2$

2. Sphere:

- Volume: $V = (\frac{4}{3})\pi r^3$ (where r is the radius of the sphere)

- Surface area: $SA = 4\pi r^2$

3. Cone:

- Volume: $V = (\frac{1}{3})\pi r^2 h$ (where r is the radius of the base and h is the height of the cone)

- Surface area: $SA = \pi r^2 + \pi r \sqrt{(r^2 + h^2)}$

4. Cylinder:

- Volume: $V = \pi r^2 h$ (where r is the radius of the base and h is the height of the cylinder)

- Surface area: $SA = 2\pi r^2 + 2\pi rh$

5. Pyramid:

- Volume: $V = (\frac{1}{3})Bh$ (where B is the area of the base and h is the height of the pyramid)

- Surface area: $SA = B + \frac{1}{2}Pl$ (where P is the perimeter of the base and l is the slant height of the pyramid)

Simplify Expressions

1. $20m + m$

2. $9 + y - 10y + 13 - 10y$

3. $8 + 6m + 7 + 12m$

4. $-5 + 6 - 10y + 15y - 3 + 11y$

5. −x − 19x

6. −15z − 5 + 13z

7. 7 + 8(4y + 14)

8. 6m − 2m + 8 + 18

9. m + 17m

10. $-5x - 10x$

11. $10y + 12y$

12. $z - 12z + 16z + 3 + 7$

13. $7z - 9 - 16z + 11$

14. $-13k - 7 - 11k$

15. $-16 - 20x + 5x - 7 + 5x$

16. $12 + 19z - 10z$

17. $17 + m - 5 + 2m$

18. $11z - 1 - 18z + 15$

19. $-4 - 8x + 18x - 5 + 2x$

20. $18m + 5m$

21. $11 + 1(10k - 12)$

22. $-15 + 2k - 12k - 6 - 4k$

23. $k + 20k$

24. $12 + 16(6z - 19)$

25. $-3x + 19x + 8 - 10x$

26. $16 + 15z - 3 + 3z - 2 + 19z$

27. $4m + 14m$

28. $8x - 15x + 1 + 19$

29. $-m + 10m$

30. $-20y + 17 + 16y + 15 + 17y - 5$

31. $16 + 18(13m + 4)$

32. $16k - 7 - 4k + 12 - 14$

33. $4 + 10x - 20 + 5x - 14 + 2x$

34. $15y + 12 - 5y + 2 + 6y + 8$

35. $-2m - 10m$

36. $13m - m$

37. $14 + 2(19y - 7)$

38. $-5m + 20 - 1 + 14m$

39. $12k + 5 - 4k + 7 + 15k + 8$

40. $18z + 2 - 3 - 15z + 20z$

41. $11 + 13(12k + 7)$

42. $-11k + 3 + 13k$

43. $-15m + 18 + 13m$

44. $-5 + 12z - 15z - 16 + 14z$

45. $2m + 15 - 12m - 20 + 18m - 20$

46. $13 + 14k + 10 + 12k$

47. $-9x + 2x$

48. $8 - 6k + 9 - 2k + 9 - 19k$

49. $12k + k$

SUMMER MATH WORKBOOK — BUILDING ACTIVITIES

Solving Equations

Evaluate each expression when: $x = 5$

1. $\dfrac{3 + 15}{x + 1} =$

2. $10x - 2 =$

3. $\dfrac{1 + 10}{x + 6} =$

4. $10 \div x =$

5. $3x - 6 + 9x =$

6. $x + 8 + x =$

7. $x + 8 + 3x =$

8. $x \div 5 =$

9. $9x + 4 =$

10. $8x + x =$

Solving Equations

Evaluate each expression when: $x = 2$

1. $x \div 2 =$

2. $7x + 5 =$

3. $4x + 6 + (2x - 10) =$

4. $2 + 8x =$

5. $9(4 - x) =$

6. $x^1 + 4x^1 =$

7. $5 + 7x =$

8. $6(2 + x) =$

9. $7x + 6 - 6x =$

10. $(9x + 9) + (10x + 10) =$

Solving Equations

Evaluate each expression when: $x = 7$

1. $x + 9 + 9x =$

2. $8 + x =$

3. $\dfrac{x}{1} =$

4. $5 + x =$

5. $7 \div x =$

6. $6x + 3 =$

7. $7^1 + x^1 =$

8. $\dfrac{35}{x} =$

9. $9x + 5 =$

10. $8x + 1 =$

Solving Equations

Evaluate each expression when: $x = 4$

1. $10 + (6x + 5) - 3 + (6x) =$

2. $(x + 6) \div 1 =$

3. $10 + \dfrac{x}{1} =$

4. $5(8 + x) =$

5. $(x)(7x) =$

6. $5 + (4x + 7) =$

7. $\dfrac{48}{x} =$

8. $x + 6 + 3x =$

9. $4x - x =$

10. $8x + 1 =$

Solving Equations

Evaluate each expression when: $x = 2$

1. $1 + \dfrac{40}{x} + 4^1 =$

2. $7x + x =$

3. $6 \div x =$

4. $x^1 + x - 1 =$

5. $3 + x =$

6. $5 - x =$

7. $(x)(7x) =$

8. $\dfrac{6 + 22}{x + 2} =$

9. $6x - 7 =$

10. $(x + 10) \div 2 =$

Equations (One Side)

Solve for the variable.

1. $1 + (3k + 16) - 19 + (17k) = 258$

2. $11z + 3 = 212$

3. $2.5 = z \div 4$

4. $(y + 14) \div 8 = 3.5$

5. $4 + (9z + 10) = 95$

6. $5k + 20 = 90$

7. $128 = 11k + 18 + (10k - 16)$

8. $6z + 10 = 76$

9. $z + 19 = 22$

10. $256 = 11m + 7m + 14m$

11. $-2 = z^2 + z - 8$

12. $1.333 = \dfrac{12 + k}{k + 8}$

13. $1.5 = (z + 12) \div 12$

14. $k + 1 - 7k = -5$

15. $y - 12 = -4$

16. $11z + z = 144$

17. $$\frac{20 + y}{y + 12} = 1.615$$

18. $342 = 8k + 10k + k$

19. $5 + x = 13$

20. $26 = 13(8 - y)$

21. $56 = 8z + 8$

22. $14 \div (m + 6) = 0.583$

23. $18m + 14 + (19m - 14) = 666$

24. $y - 9 = 9$

25. $16 + \dfrac{z}{20} = 17$

26. $(3k + 12) + (7k - 15) = 177$

27. $9 + \dfrac{6 + k}{5k} - 10 = -0.720$

28. $45 = 2z^2 + 3z^2$

29. $140 = 9m + m$

30. $x + 6 = 10$

31. $2.625 = (z + 6) \div 8$

32. $33,124 = (13y)^2$

33. $1 = (x)^2$

34. $7 = 6 \div y + 6$

35. $260 = 15y + 20$

36. $32 = 14 + y$

37. $12 \div y = 1$

38. $17(4 - k) = -204$

39. $170 = 10(1 + m)$

40. $600 = 9y^2 + 15y^2$

Equations (Two Sides)

Solve for the variable.

1. $17 - k = 2k + 8$

2. $6x + 5 = 47 - x$

3. $54 - 7z = 9z + 6$

4. $5 + 5k + 4 = 9 + k + 4$

5. $36 - k = 5 + 2k + 7$

6. $3 + 2k = 21 - k$

7. $12 + m = 6m + 2$

8. $4m + 7 = 25 + m$

9. $3 + 6x + 9 = 27 + x + 0$

10. $6k + 2 = 3k + 26$

11. $5 + 8x + 3 = 19 - x + 7$

12. $35 - x = 6 + 7x + 5$

13. $8y + 4 = 18 + 6y$

14. $30 - k = 6 + 2k$

15. $55 - 2z = 7z + 1$

16. $94 - 7x = 8x + 4$

17. $36 + x + -1 = 8 + 3x + 9$

18. $73 - 3z = 6z + 1$

19. $7 + 7z = 34 + 4z$

20. $3 + 2m + 4 = 15 + m$

21. $33 + x = 9 + 7x$

22. $30 - x = 3 + 2x$

23. $8 + 2x + 6 = 20 + x + 0$

24. $17 + k = 2k + 8$

25. $44 - k = 7k + 4$

26. $15 - z = 3 + 3z + 4$

27. $39 - x = 3x + 7$

28. $10 + 2y = 5 + 3y$

29. $9 + 2z + 1 = 11 + z$

30. $7 + 7z = 3z + 19$

31. $9 + 6k = 7k + 5$

32. $2k + 4 = 1 + 3k$

33. $17 + y = 9 + 2y + 4$

34. $4 + 7z = 58 + z$

35. $4z + 14 = 8z + 6$

36. $23 + m + 1 = 9 + 2m + 8$

37. $3x + 45 = 9x + 3$

38. $48 - y + 13 = 6 + 6y + 6$

39. $9 + 7k = 22 - 6k$

40. $43 - z + 10 = 3 + 5z + 8$

41. $6 + 5x = 54 - 3x$

42. $9 + 6y = 23 - y$

43. $28 - m + 10 = 6 + 5m + 8$

44. $9y + 3 = 8 + 8y$

45. $6 + 2z = 7 + z$

46. $48 + z + \text{-}3 = 8 + 5z + 5$

47. $8z + 3 = 3z + 23$

48. $9k + 6 = 61 - 2k$

Verbal Algebra Expressions

1. Five times a number decreased by 3 is 7. Find the number.

2. Four times a number equals 36 less than eight times the number. What is the number?

3. Two-fourths of a number increased by 5 is 13. What is the number?

4. Five more than seven times a number is 33. What is the number?

5. Nine times the difference of 12 minus a number is 18. What is the number?

6. One-half of a number is 4. Find the number.

7. The sum of two numbers is 20. The difference of the same two numbers is eight. Find the numbers.

8. The sum of three numbers is 21. The largest number is five times the smallest, and the smallest is seven less than the middle number. Find the numbers.

9. One less than five times a number is 49. Find the number.

10. Three times the sum of a number and three times the number is 108. Find the number.

11. Two times the difference of 9 minus a number is 2. What is the number?

12. Two-thirds of a number decreased by 1 is 3. Find the number.

13. Find two consecutive odd integers such that eight times the larger decreased by the smaller is 37.

14. Twice a number is 4. What is the number?

15. The sum of the first and third of three consecutive numbers is 10. Find the numbers.

16. Seven times the sum of a number and two times the number is 126. Find the number.

17. Nine is equal to the quotient of a number and 8. Find the number.

18. The quotient of a number and four is 3. Find the number.

19. The sum of the first and third of three consecutive numbers is 4. Find the numbers.

20. One number is 10 more than another number. The sum of four times the larger number and three times the smaller is 103. What are the numbers?

21. One-half of a number is 1. Find the number.

22. Find two consecutive odd integers such that seven times the larger decreased by the smaller is 44.

23. Two more than three times a number is 38. What is the number?

24. One number is 8 more than another number. The sum of six times the larger number and nine times the smaller is 168. What are the numbers?

25.   A number increased by six is 10. Find the number.

26.   Two more than five times a number is equal to the number increased by 14. What is the number?

27.   One number is four times another. Their sum is 30. Find the numbers.

28.   One of two numbers is four more than the other. The sum of the numbers is 20. Find the numbers.

29. The product of ten and a number is 70. What is the number?

30. 10 is equal to the product of ten and some number. Find the number.

31. The difference of a number and seven is equal to 9. What is the number?

32. A number decreased by 1 is 6. Find the number.

33. The quotient of a number and four is 6. Find the number.

Standard Linear Equations

1. $9x + 2 = -16$

2. $5x + 9 = 59$

3. $-4x + 1 = 37$

4. $-8x + -1 = -1$

5. $10x + 2 = 32$

6. $7x + -5 = 16$

7. $-3x + -3 = -21$

8. $-8x + -6 = 34$

9. -1x + -5 = -7

13. -4x + 8 = 24

10. -8x + -4 = 36

14. 10x + -3 = 37

11. -4x + -9 = 11

15. -8x + 5 = 21

12. 10x + 3 = 53

16. -3x + -10 = 17

17. -8x + -7 = 9

21. 4x + -10 = -2

18. -3x + -7 = 14

22. 2x + 9 = -5

19. 1x + 1 = 5

23. 9x + -3 = -30

20. -2x + 3 = 3

24. 7x + 3 = 31

Find Slope from Two Points

1. (-7, -15) and (-4, -6)

2. (-3, -3) and (5, -11)

3. (-3, 0) and (2, 10)

4. (-7, 14) and (-6, 13)

5. (-3, 2) and (-2, -2)

6. (7, -47) and (10, -65)

7. (-2, -15) and (9, 84)

8. (7, -12) and (-8, 3)

9. (0, 1) and (9, 10)

13. (2, 18) and (0, 8)

10. (0, -8) and (1, -11)

14. (-4, 26) and (-3, 20)

11. (10, 87) and (0, -3)

15. (-10, -43) and (6, 37)

12. (6, 9) and (-10, -7)

16. (-10, -50) and (1, 5)

System of Equations

1. $1x + 5y = 8$

   $7x + 4y = 4$

2. $8x + 8y = 8$

   $4x + 5y = 8$

3. $5x + 6y = 8$

   $7x + 9y = 9$

4. 8x + 3y = 4

   4x + 4y = 2

5. 7x + 3y = 4

   6x + 8y = 4

6. 2x + 1y = 5

   2x + 8y = 4

7. $4x + 6y = 9$

$1x + 5y = 4$

8. $10x + 9y = 4$

$6x + 10y = 7$

9. $6x + 10y = 9$

$5x + 2y = 1$

10. $8x + 6y = 1$

$7x + 2y = 6$

11. $6x + 10y = 2$

$5x + 2y = 6$

12. $10x + 2y = 9$

$10x + 6y = 3$

Quadratic Equations

1. $5n^2 - 12n - 9 = 0$

2. $5r^2 - 7r - 12 = 0$

3. $8n^2 - 10n - 19 = 0$

4. $4k^2 + 5k - 75 = 0$

5. $-5x^2 + 6x + 4 = 0$

6. $4x^2 - 9 = 0$

7. $-9n^2 + 8n + 24 = 0$

8. $r^2 + 8r - 22 = -8$

9. $-5k^2 - 10k - 6 = -3$

13. $2x^2 - x - 100 = 5$

10. $-5a^2 + 4a + 14 = -6$

14. $4n^2 - 3n - 34 = -10$

11. $12k^2 - 7k - 24 = -2$

15. $-11m^2 = -4$

12. $11x^2 - 24 = -7$

16. $3v^2 + 8v = 28$

17. $-4n^2 - 3n = -1$

18. $-3v^2 - 11 = 0$

19. $-a^2 - 9 = -6a$

20. $-3n^2 + 32 = 4n$

Distributing and Combining Terms

1. $-6b - 5 + 1 + 4b$

2. $3p - 5p$

3. $-6 - 2x + x - 6$

4. $-7(2x - 1)$

5. $4(4 + 4b)$

6. $-10(9b + 2)$

7. $-3(k + 6) + 4$

8. $-2 - 10(8n + 1)$

9. $-4(x - 5) - 5$

13. $-8(7a + 2) - 6a(2a - 4)$

10. $-2(-5k - 9) + 4(8 - 9k)$

14. $6n(n + 6) + 7n(3n - 5)$

11. $8(b + 2) - 5(b + 6)$

15. $5v(4v + 8) + 5(7 + 4v)$

12. $6(4x + 5) - 5(x - 8)$

16. $-3(-8x - 2) - 4(7x + 4)$

17. -7(6 - 2n) - 6(8n - 8)

18. -7(b + 5) - (7b + 2)

Factoring with special cases

1. $8x^2 + 32$

2. $27v^3 + 24v$

3. $16p + 2$

4. $40x^2 + 30x$

5. $10ab^2 + 40a^3$

6. $7xy - 21$

7. $14x^2y^3 + 10x^3$

8. $10y^4 + 20x^3$

9. $48k^3 + 30k + 60$

13. $-14 + 63mn + 70m^4$

10. $81m^5 + 54m^4 + 63m^3$

14. $45xy^2 + 18x^2y - 45x^2y^2$

11. $4b^2 - 18b + 10$

15. $30y^3x^2 - 40y^5 + 10y^3x$

12. $-10r^3 + 15r^2 - 15r$

16. $-21u^3v^2 + 21u^3v + 12uv$

17. $16r^2 - 25$

18. $16a^2 - 1$

19. $9v^2 - 25$

20. $9x^2 - 4$

21. $n^2 + 8n + 16$

22. $16x^2 - 40x + 25$

23. $4a^2 - 4a + 1$

24. $16x^2 + 8x + 1$

25. $x^4 + 4x^2 + 4$

26. $n^4 + 10n^2 + 25$

27. $25x^4 + 30x^2 + 9$

28. $16 p^4 - 25$

Polynomials

1. $(5n + 4n^2) + (8n - 4n^2)$

5. $(4x - 4x^3) + (7x^3 - 3x + 5x^2)$

2. $(8n3 - n) - (4n^3 - 6n)$

6. $(3x^2 + 3x) - (4x^2 + 7x + 4)$

3. $(b^3 - 7b) + (8b - 8b^3)$

7. $(6 p^4 + 6) - (3 - 7 p^4 - 3 p^3)$

4. $(7x^4 + 2x) + (5x - x^4)$

8. $(8x + 1) + (6x + 4x^2 - 5)$

9. $(5x^2 - 6 - 5x^4) + (5x^4 - 3 - 6x^2)$

11. $(7n^2 - 8n - 6) - (4 - 3n - 2n^2)$

10. $(a^4 + 4 - 4a) - (8a^4 + 2 - 5a)$

12. $(6 + 7m - 4m^3) + (8m - 7m^3 - 2)$

13. $(7m - 7n)(4m - 2n)$

14. $(2a - 7b)(4a - 7b)$

15. $(x + 3y)(6x - 8y)$

16. $(3m - 3n)(3m + 3n)$

17. $(3x + 2y)(4x^2 + xy - 2y^2)$

18. $(5x - 7y)(3x^2 + 4xy - 4y^2)$

19. $(6u - 3v)(6u^2 + 4uv - 6v^2)$

20. $(7m - 2n)(7m^2 - mn + 8n^2)$

21. $(6u^2 + 6uv + v^2)(6u^2 + 5uv - 6v^2)$

22. $(5a^2 - 2ab + 8b^2)(5a^2 + 3ab + 4b^2)$

23. $(2x^2 + 4xy + 7y^2)(5x^2 - xy + 8y^2)$

24. $(2x^2 + xy + 6y^2)(6x^2 + 5xy + 4y^2)$

Area and Perimeter

1.

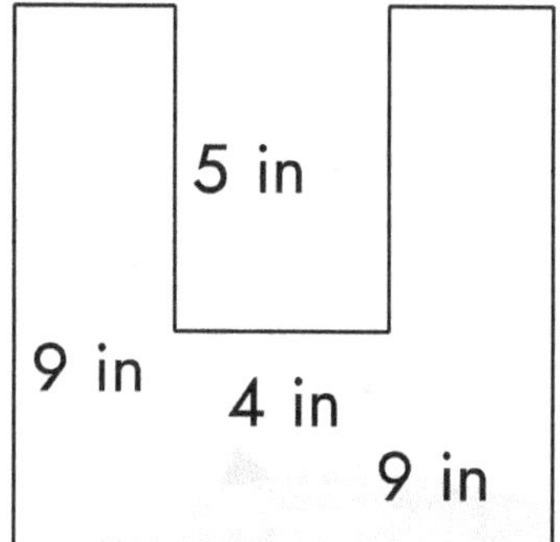

2.

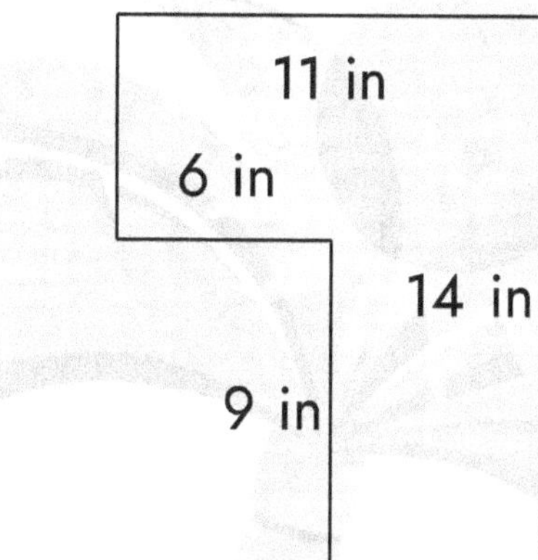

3.

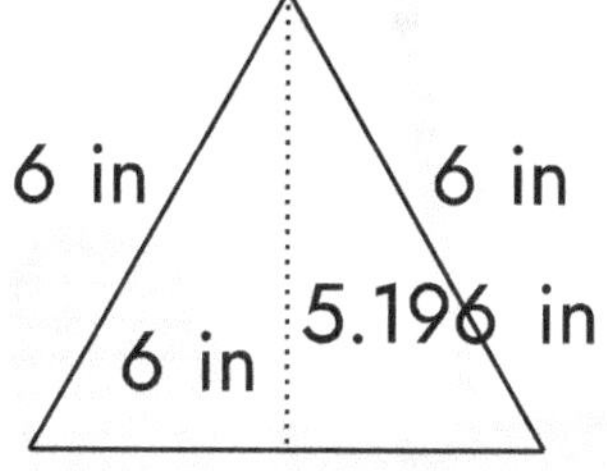

4.

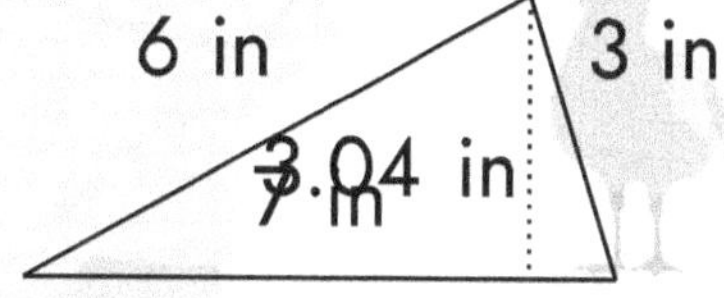

5.

12 in
12 in
12 in
10.392 in

6.

8 in
13 in
4 in
13 in

7.

9 in
12 in
5 in
10 in

8.

7 in
7 in
6.32 in
6 in

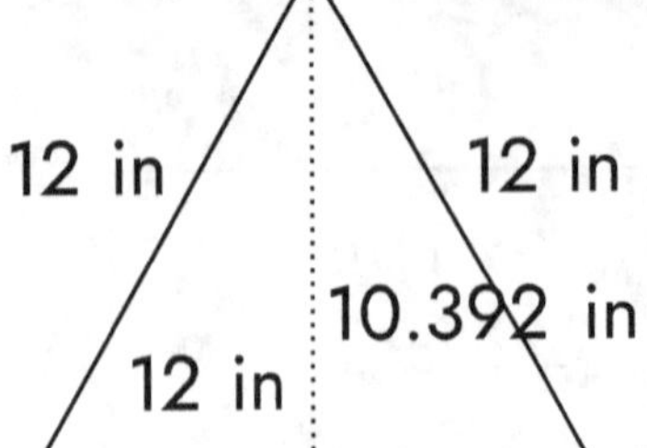

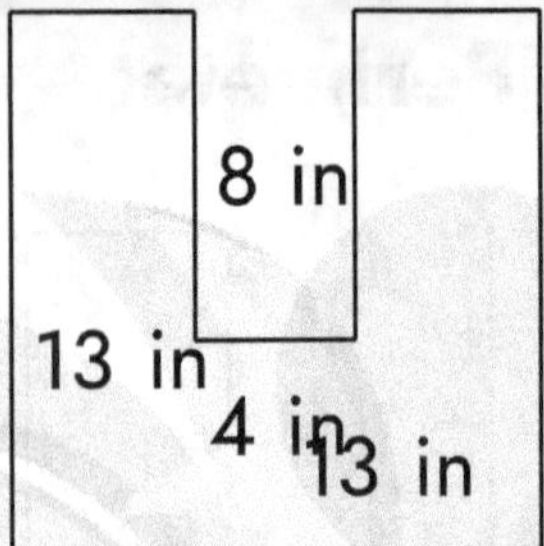

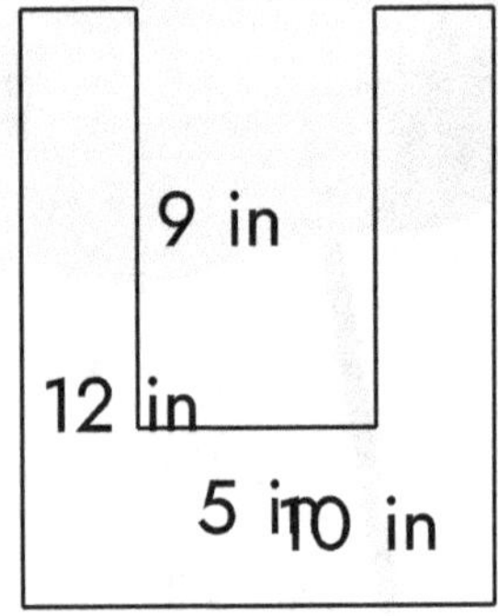

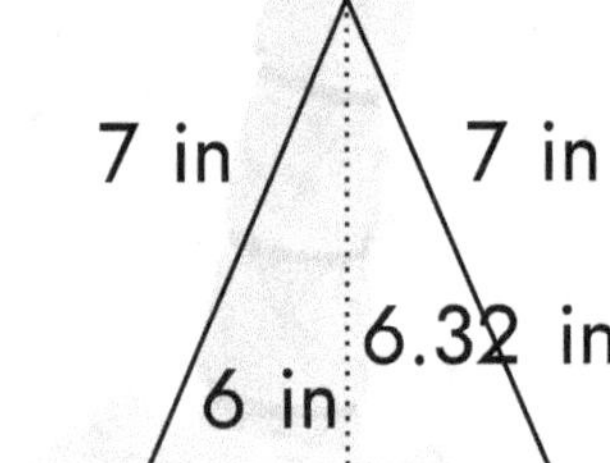

NAME:

9.

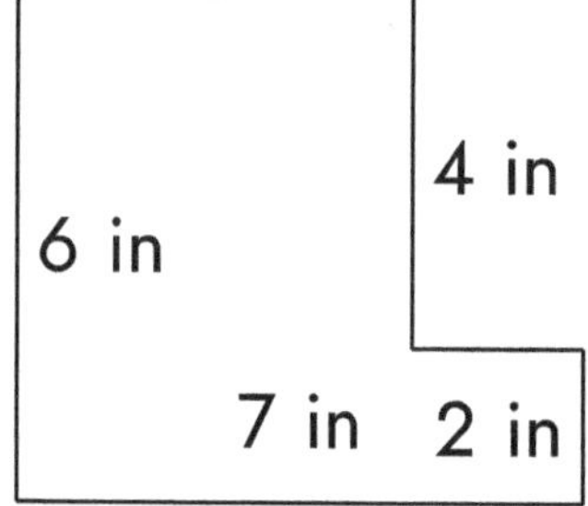

10.

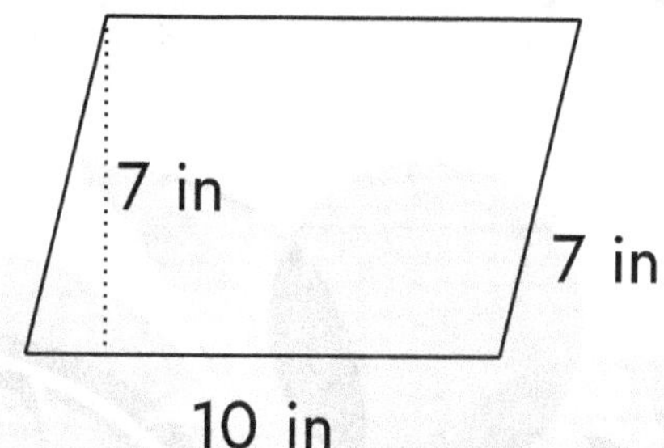

11.

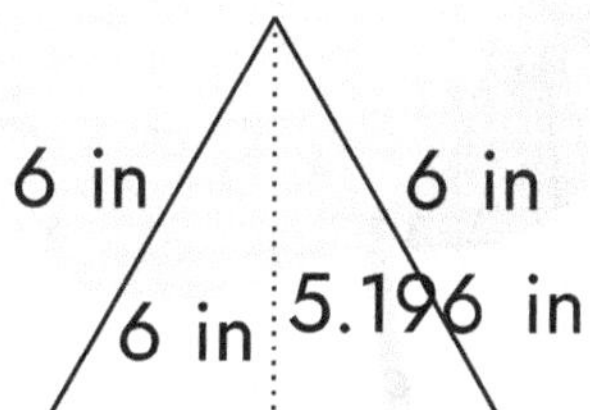

12.

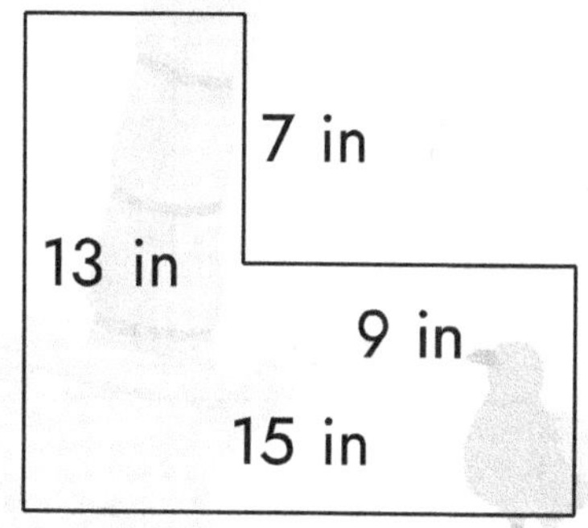

13.

9 in
6 in
4.00 in

14.

12 in
12 in
10.392 in
12 in

15.

4 in
5 in
4 in
7 in

16.

11 in
11 in
10.80 in
4 in

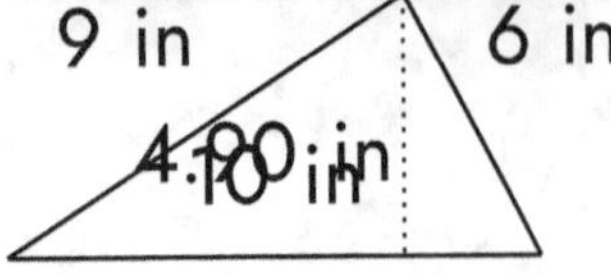

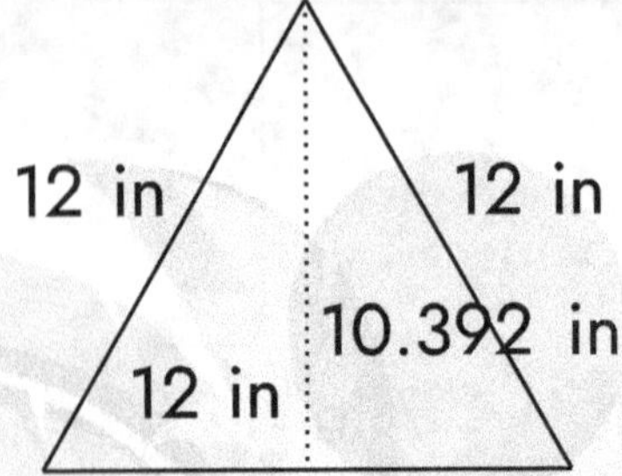

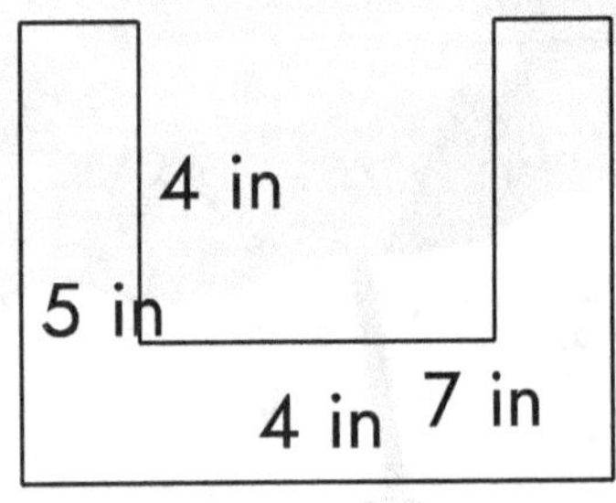

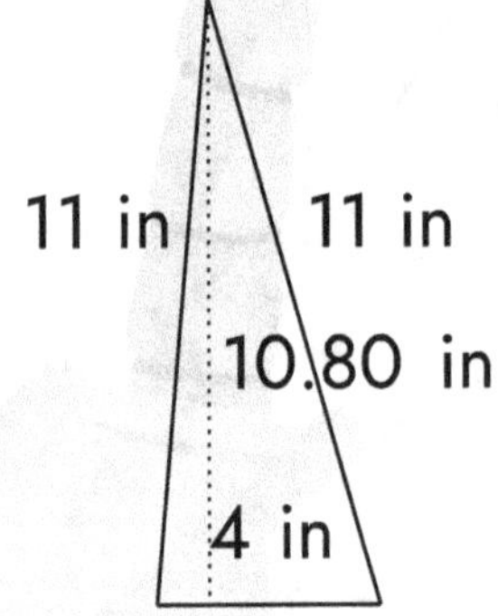

17.

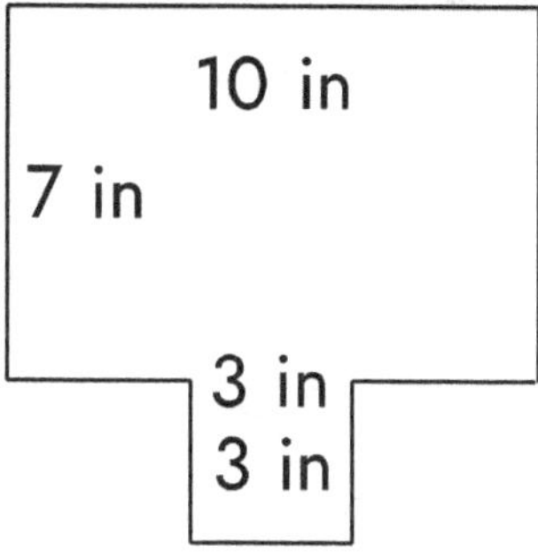

10 in

7 in

3 in

3 in

18.

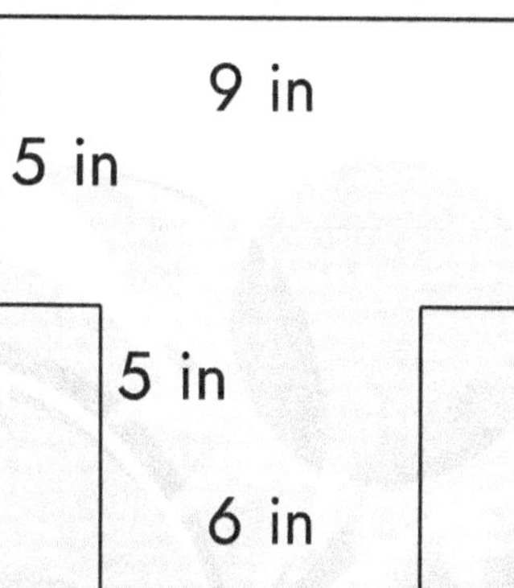

9 in

5 in

5 in

6 in

19.

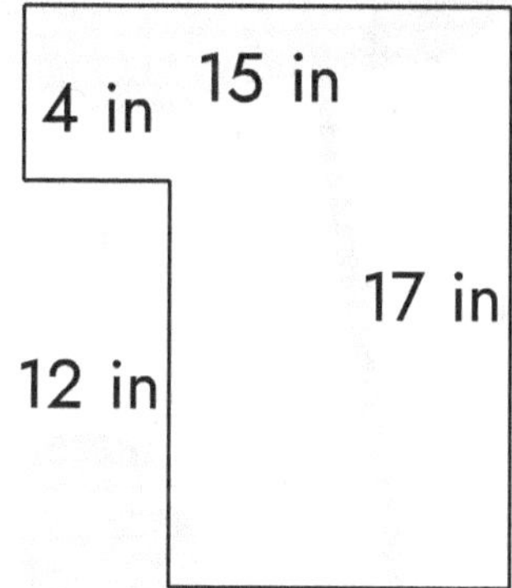

4 in

15 in

17 in

12 in

20.

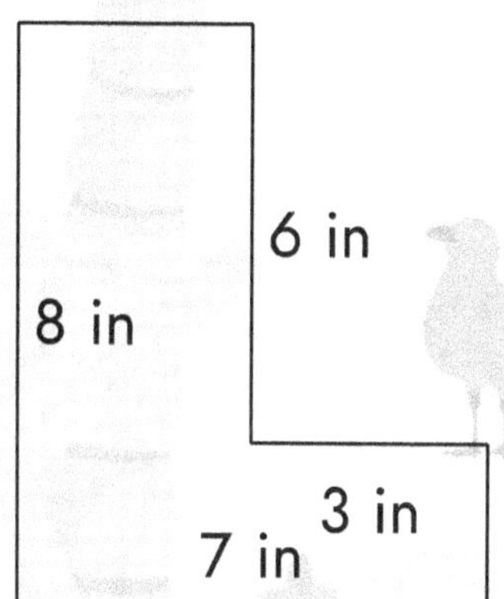

6 in

8 in

3 in

7 in

21.   4 in   6 in   3.45 in   8 in

22.   14 in   14 in   12 in

23.   6 in   11 in   6 in   15 in

24.   4 in   6 in   6 in   6 in   7 in

25.

8 in
7 in
5 in
5 in

26.

7 in
3 in
5 in
2 in

27.

15 in
15 in
13.75 in
12 in

28.

14 in
14 in
12.87 in
11 in

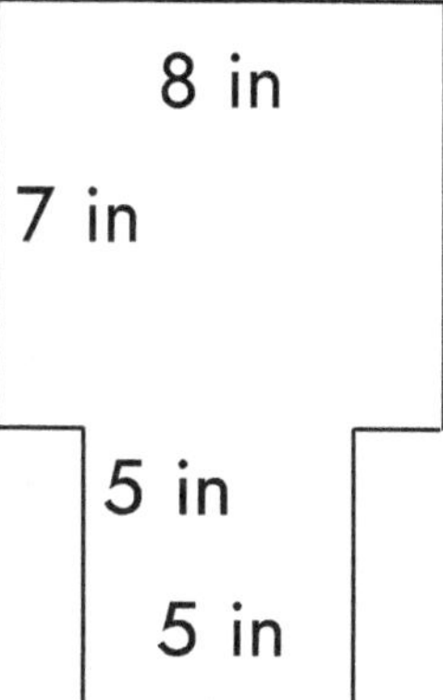

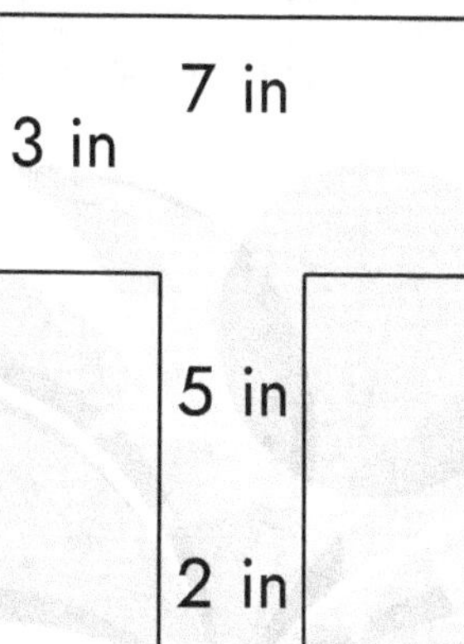

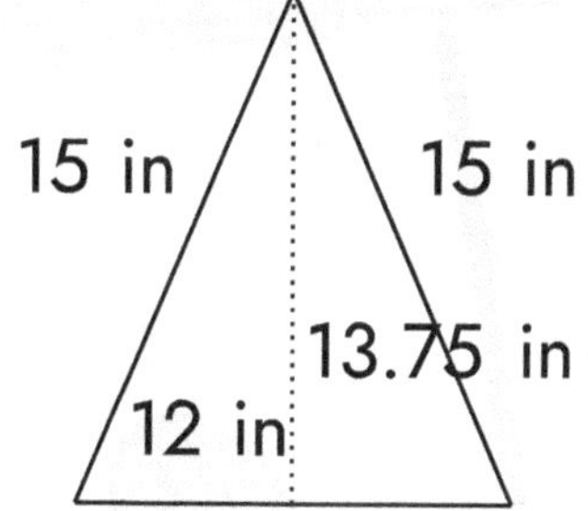

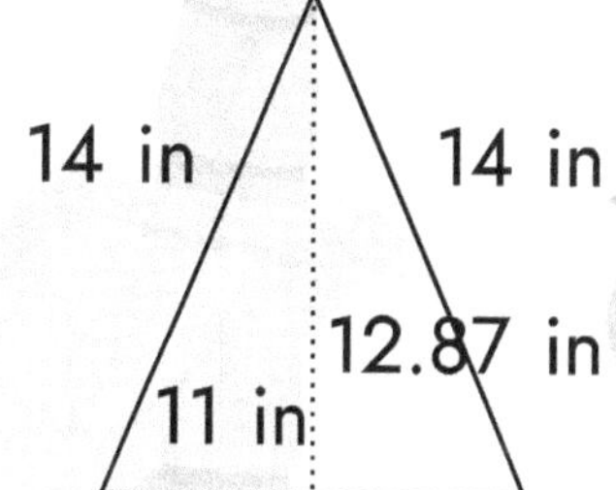

Volume and Surface Area

29.

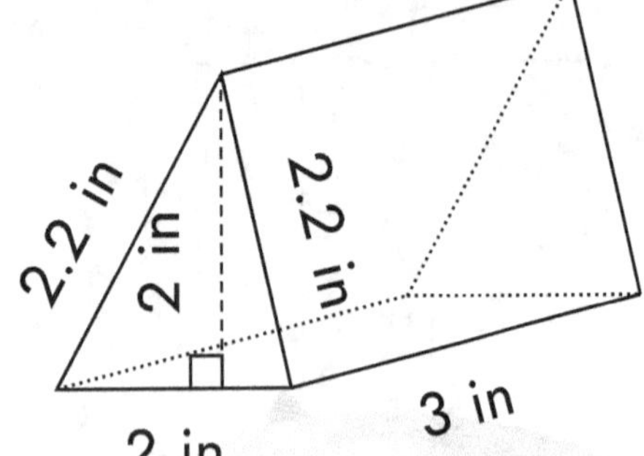

30.

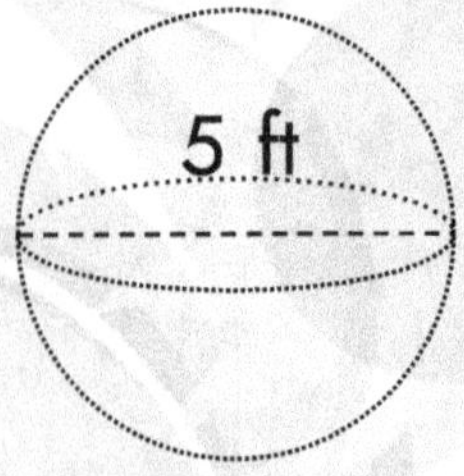

31.

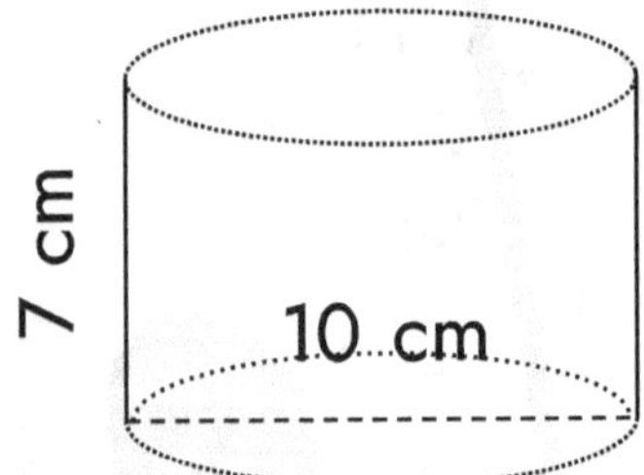

32.

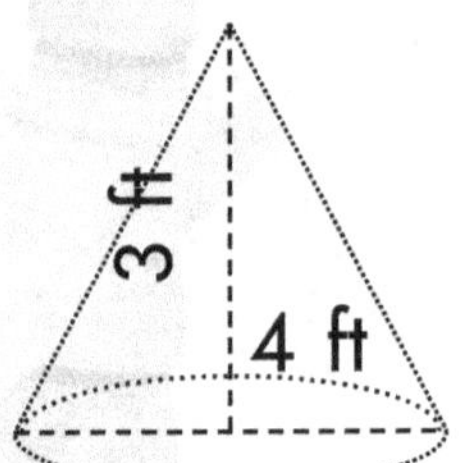

33.

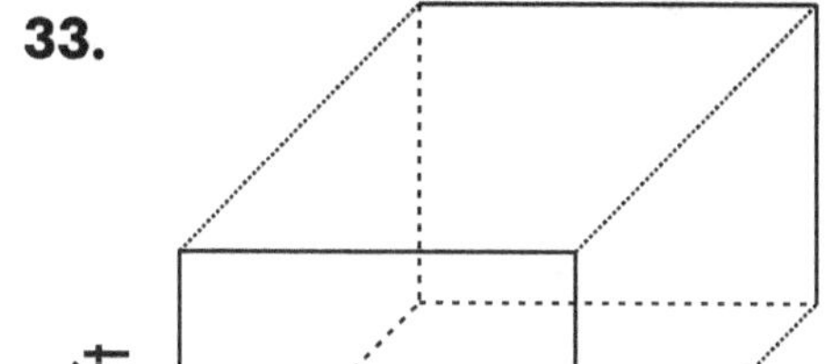

34.

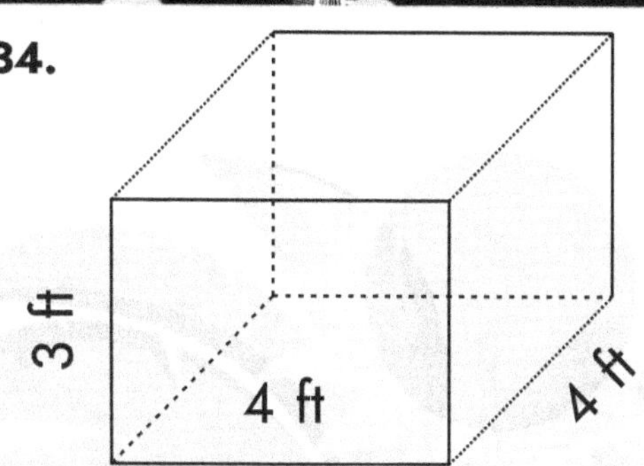

35.

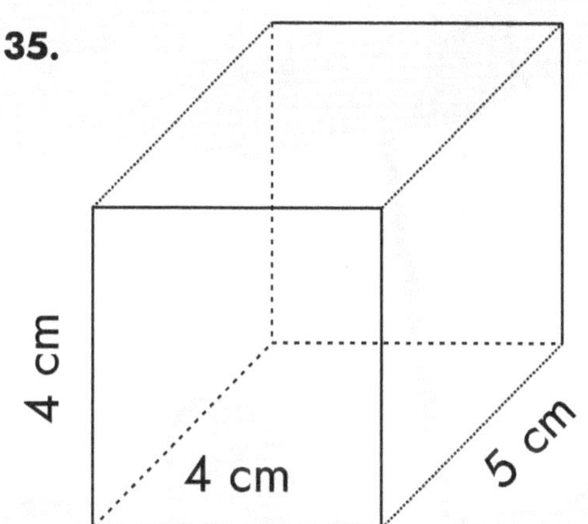

36.

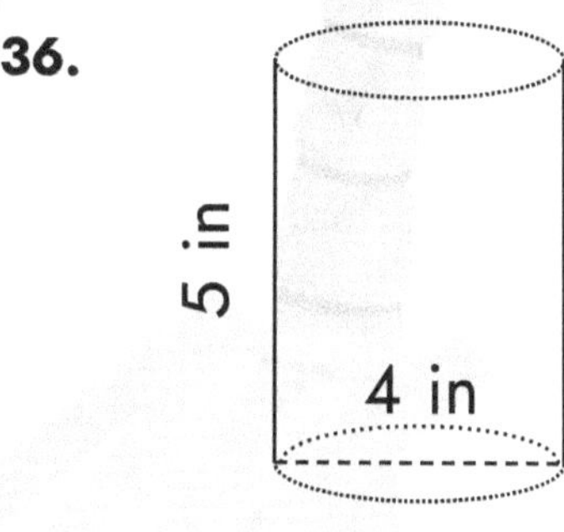

37.

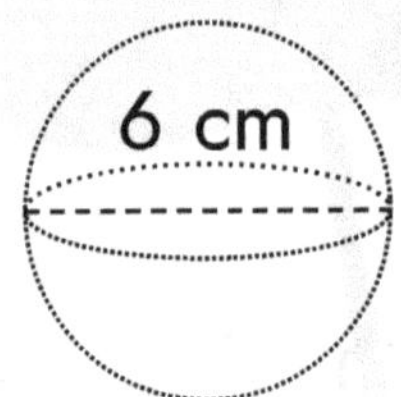

38.

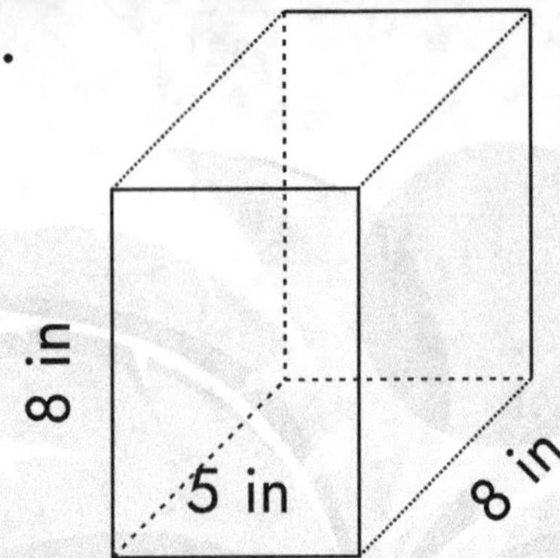

39.

40.

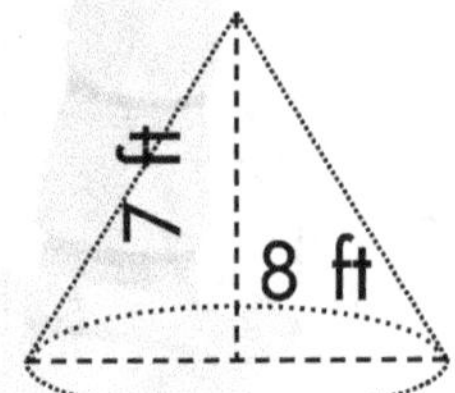

41.

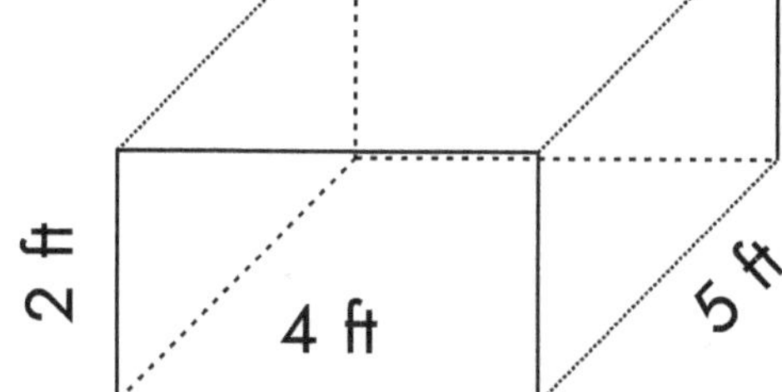

42.

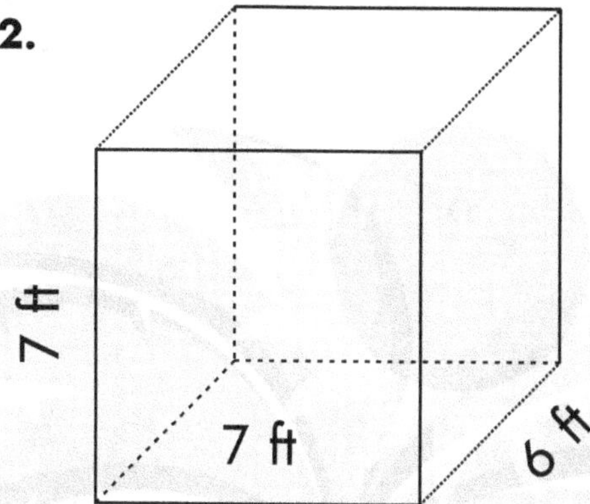

43.

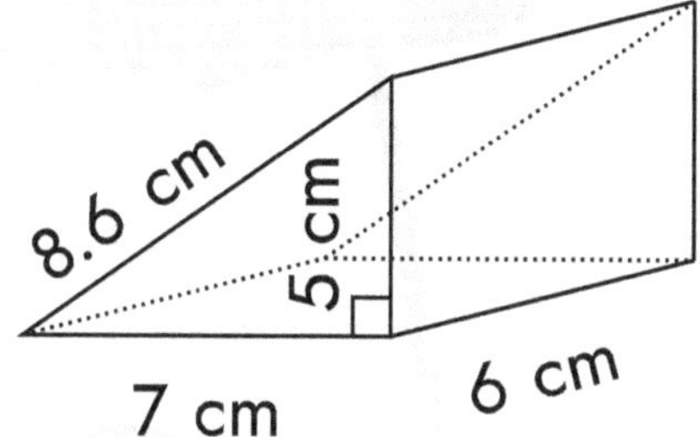

44.

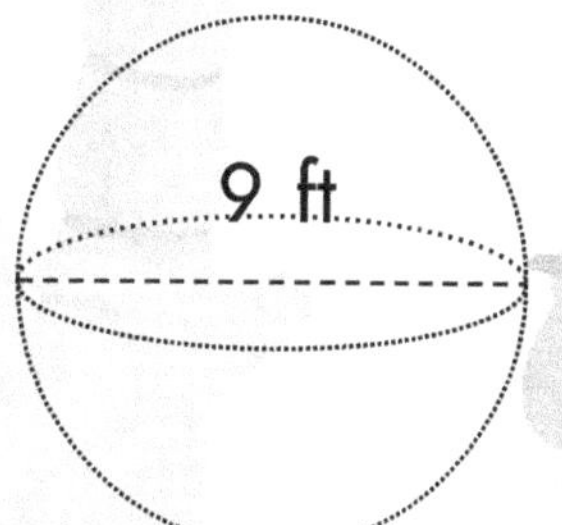

SUMMER MATH WORKBOOK
NAME:
BUILDING ACTIVITIES

45.

7 ft
6 ft

46.

5.4 cm
7.8 cm
5 cm
8 cm
9 cm

47.

3 cm
3 cm
4 cm

48.

4 in
4 in
3 in

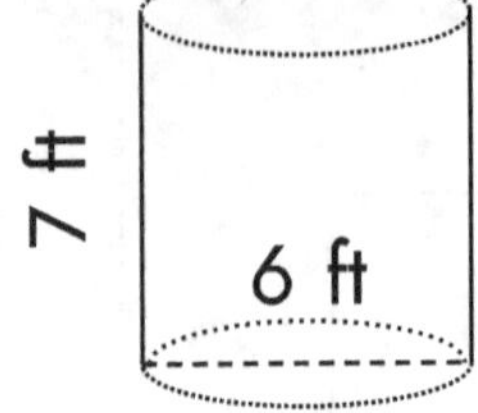

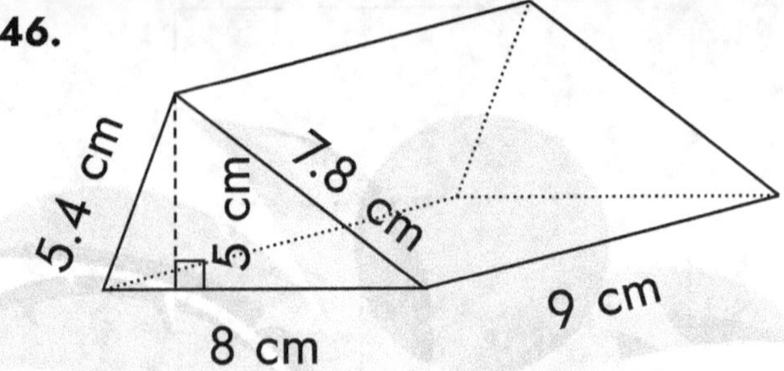

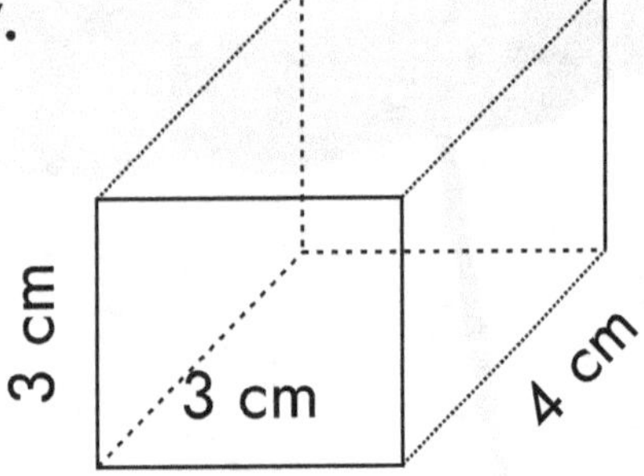

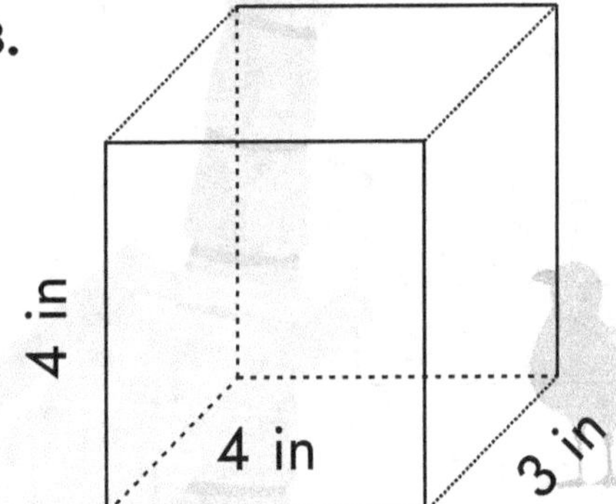

49.

4.5 ft
4 ft
4.5 ft
4 ft
3 ft

50.

2.2 ft
2 ft
2.2 ft
2 ft
3 ft

51.

3.6 cm
3 cm
3.6 cm
4 cm
5 cm

52.

8 ft
8 ft

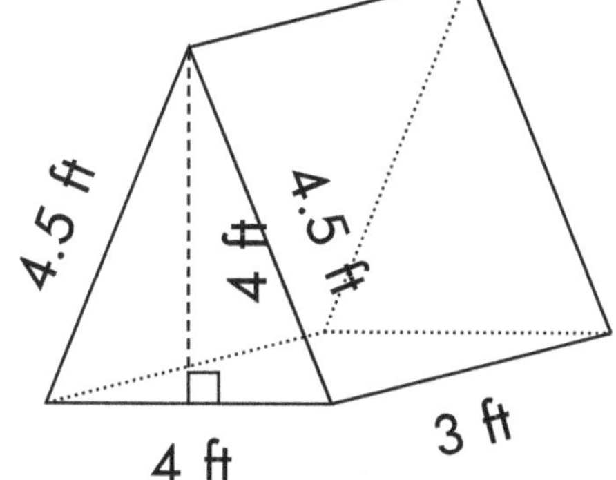

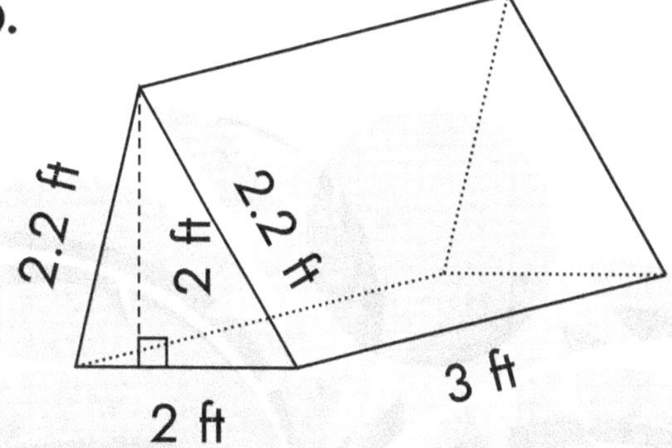

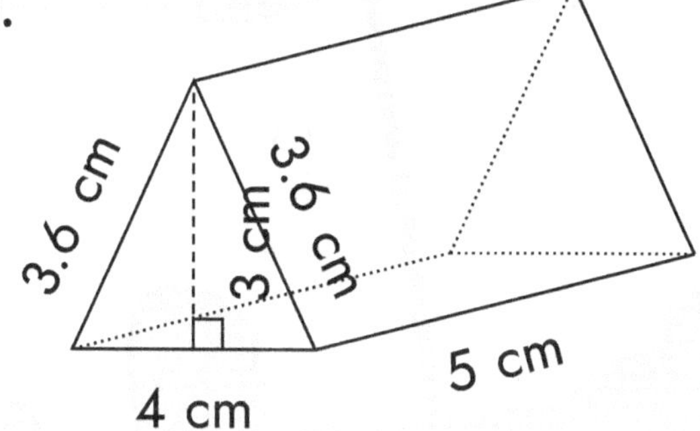

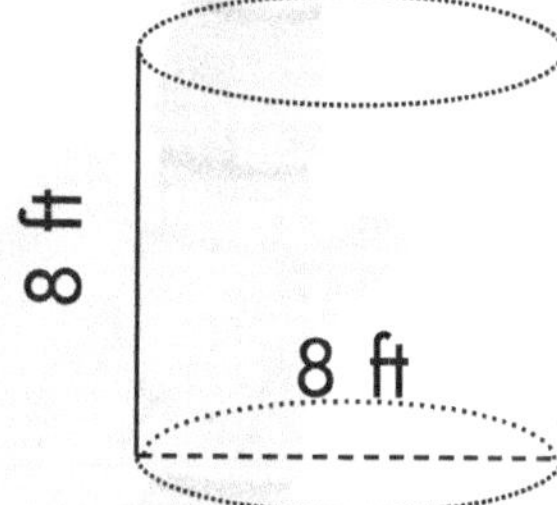

SUMMER MATH WORKBOOK
NAME:
BUILDING ACTIVITIES

53.

9 cm
6 cm

54.

6 cm
6 cm

55.

4 in
4 in
3 in

56.

3 in
2 in

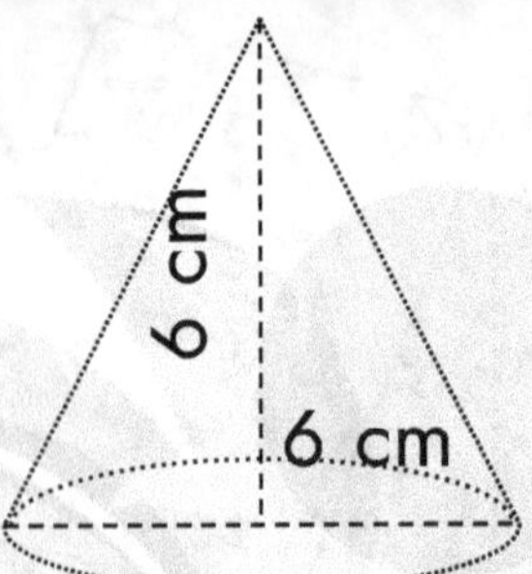

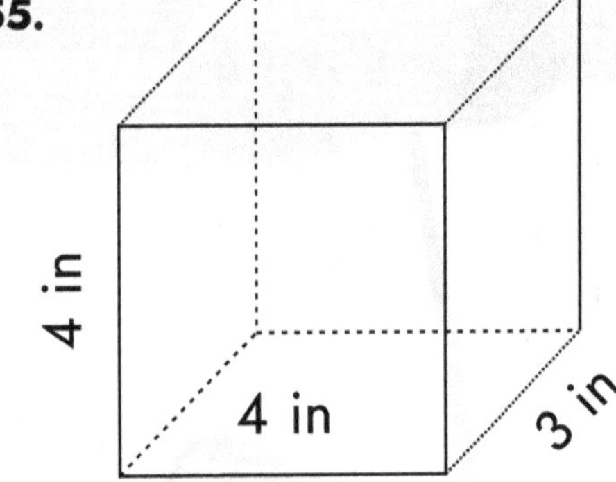

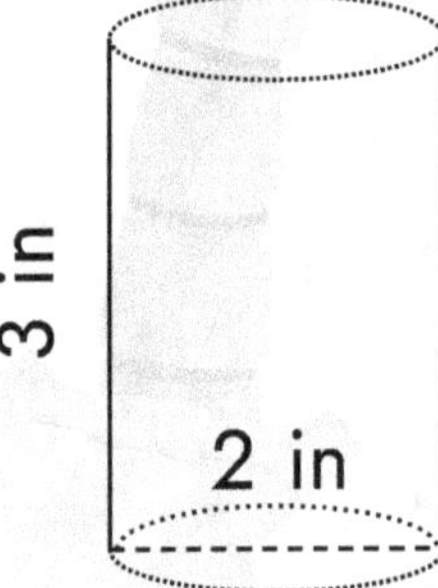

Pythagorean Theorem

57. 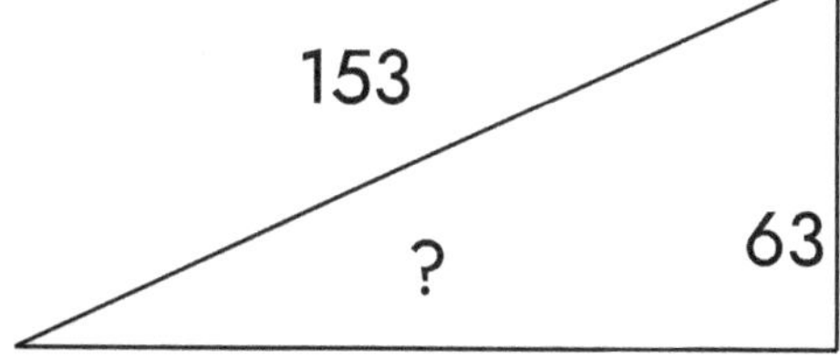

58. 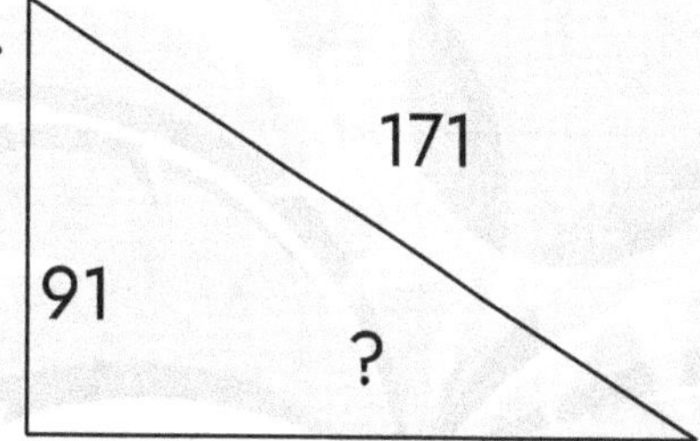

59. 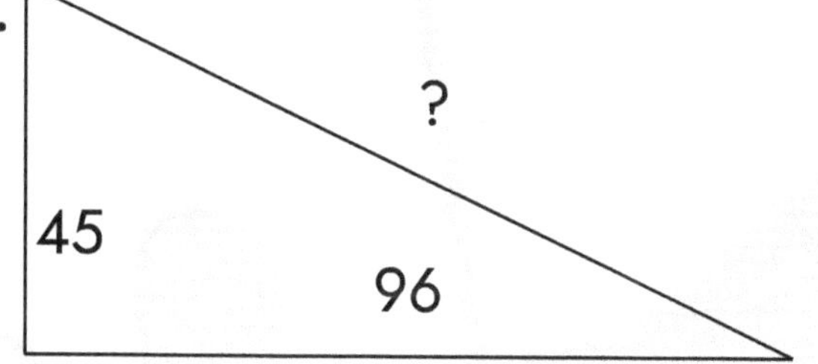

60. 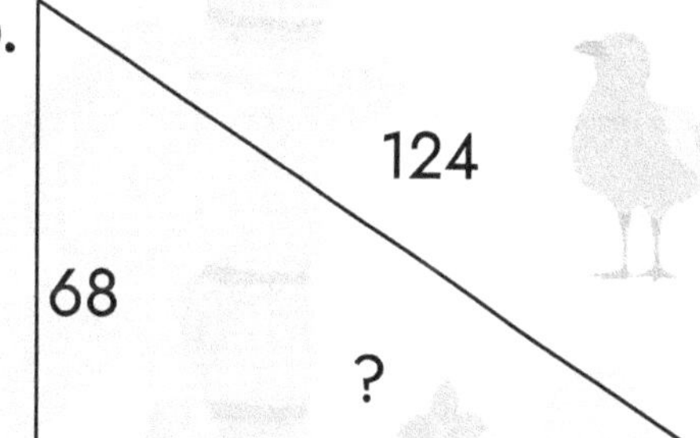

61.

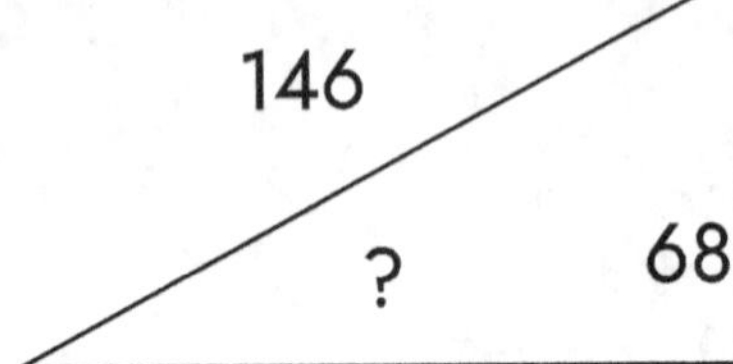

62.

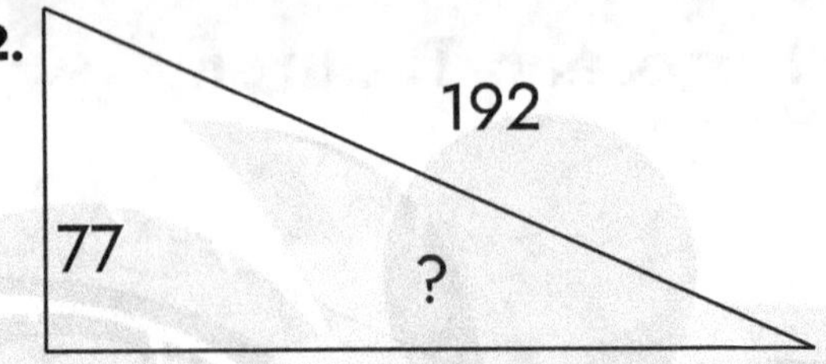

63.

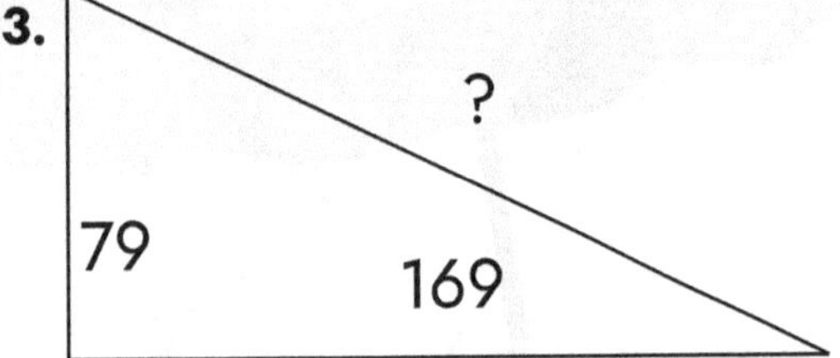

64.

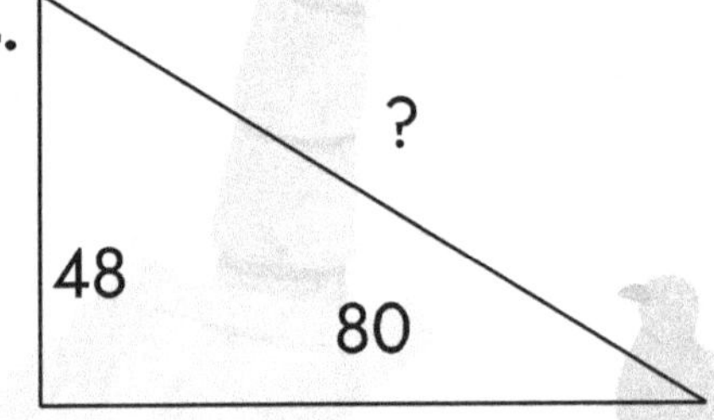

65.

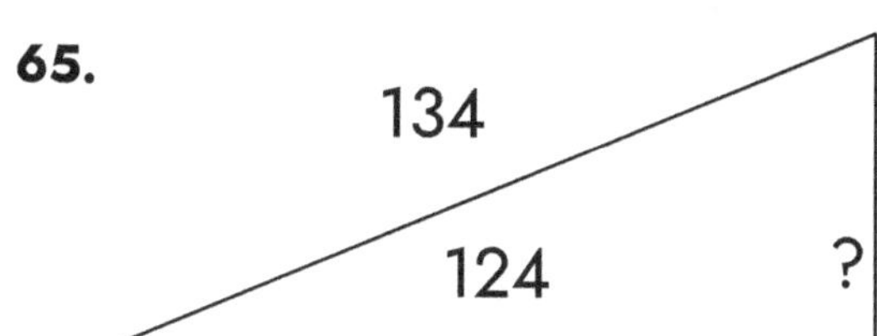

66.

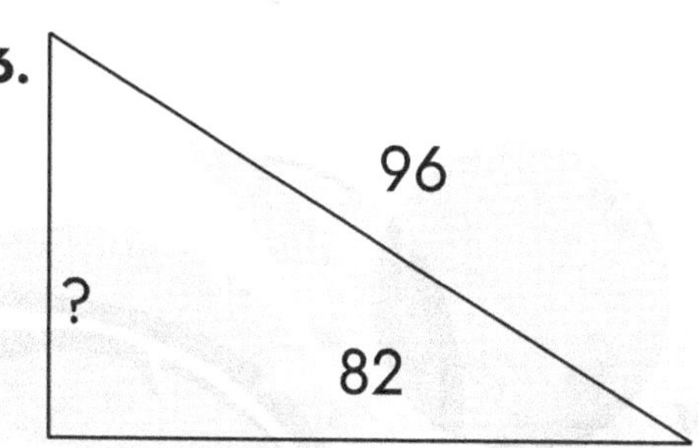

67.

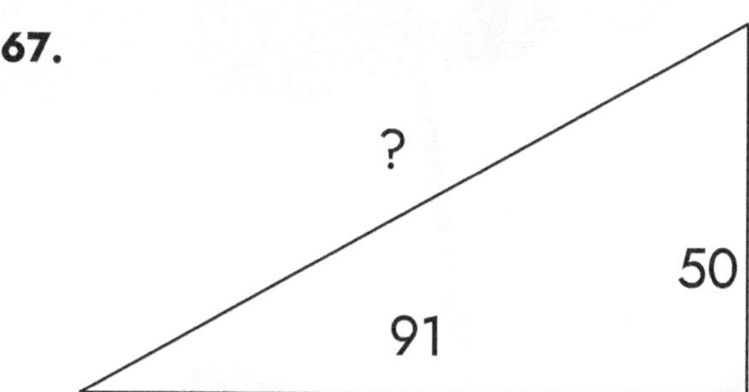

68.

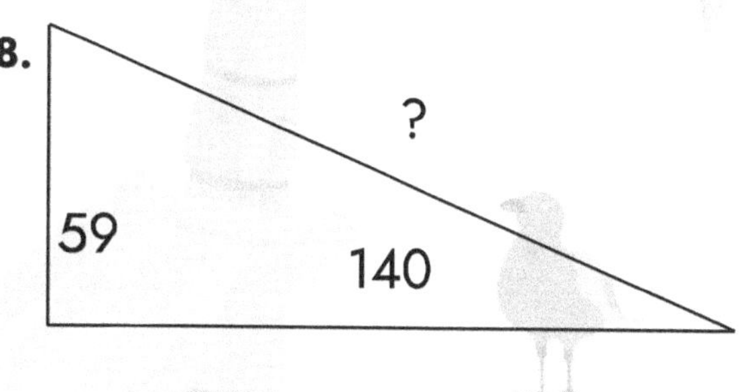

69.

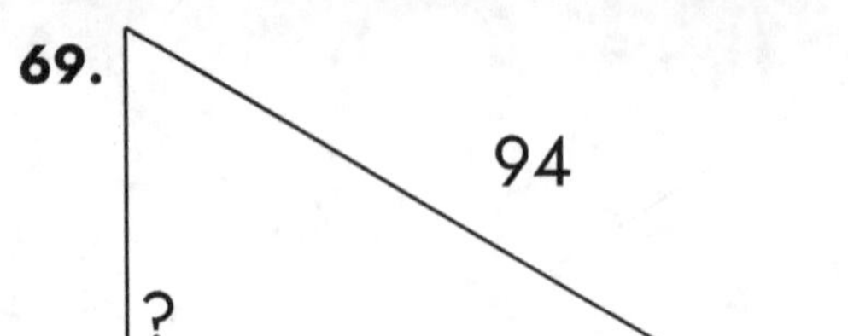

70.

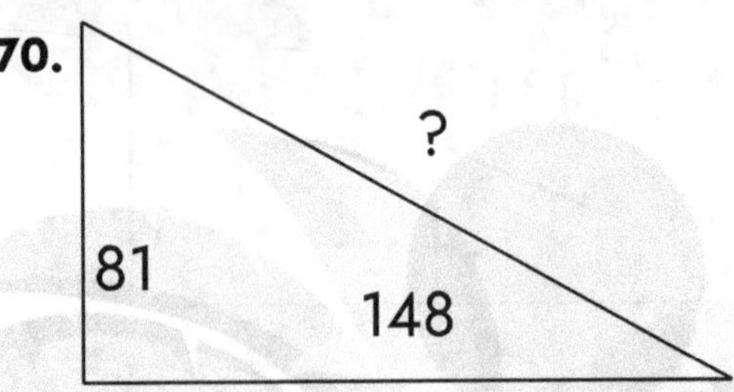

71.

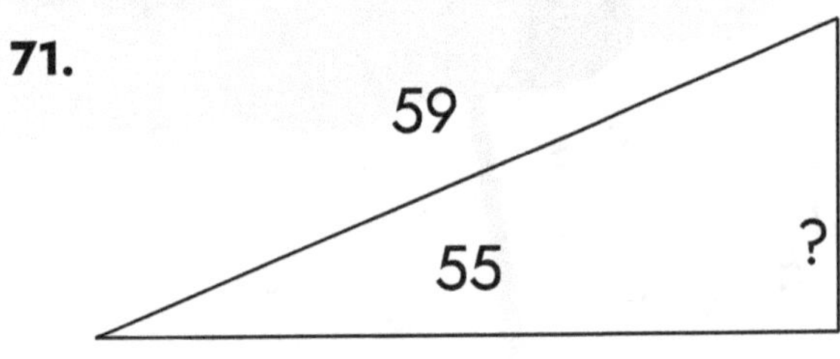

72.

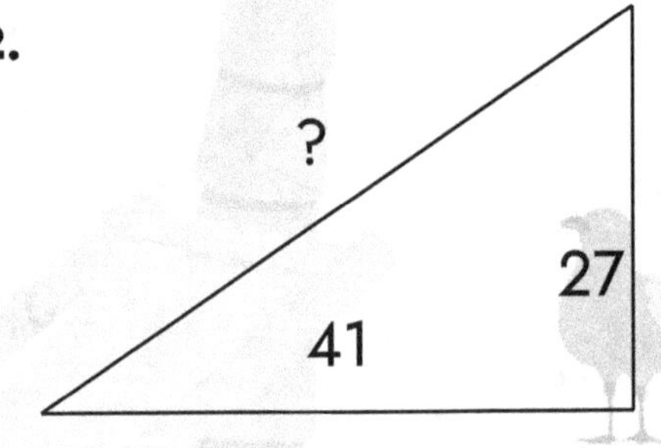

73.

30

?

58

74.

126

110

?

75.

?

154

66

76.

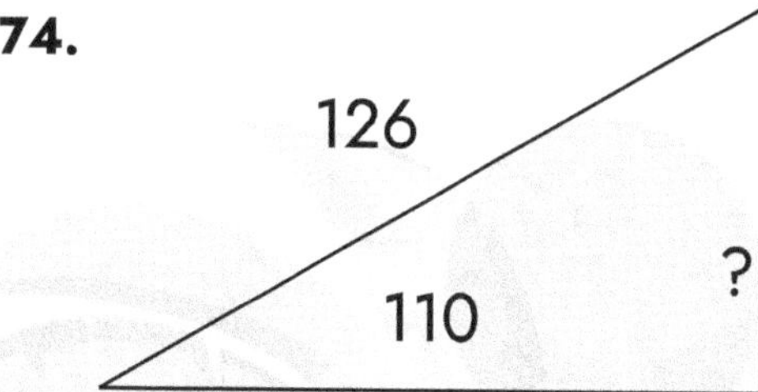

134

?

67

77.

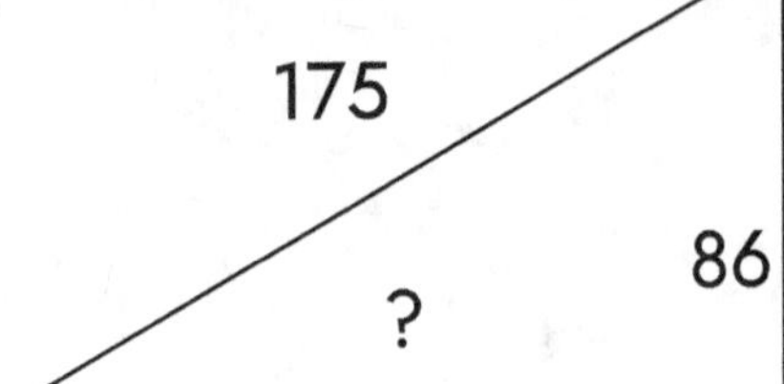

78.

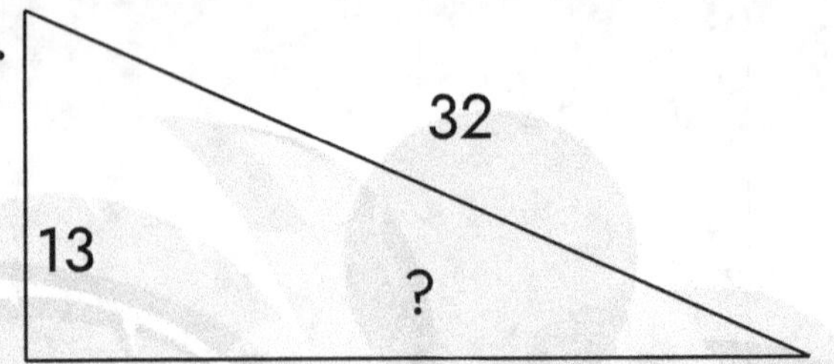

79.

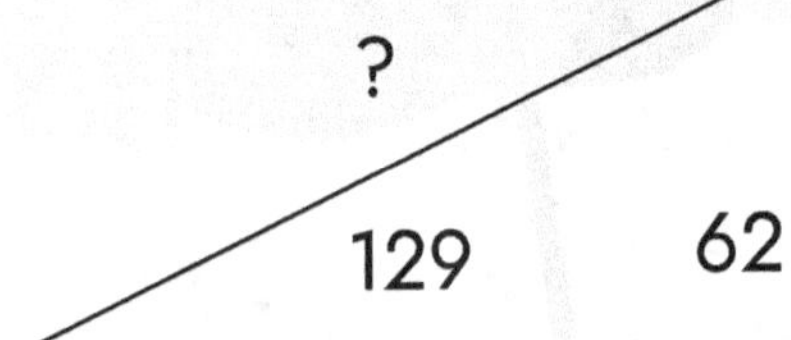

80.

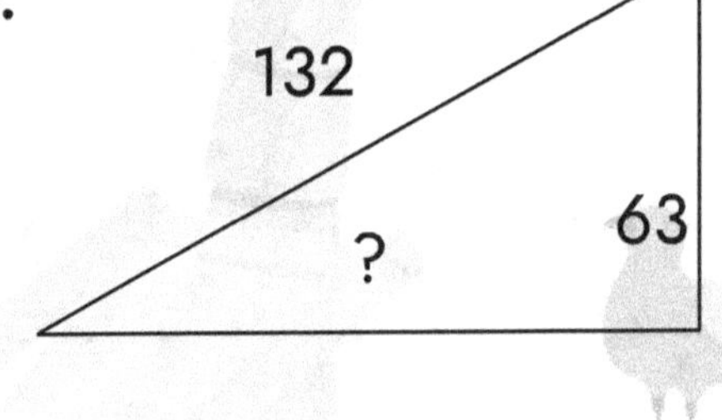

81.

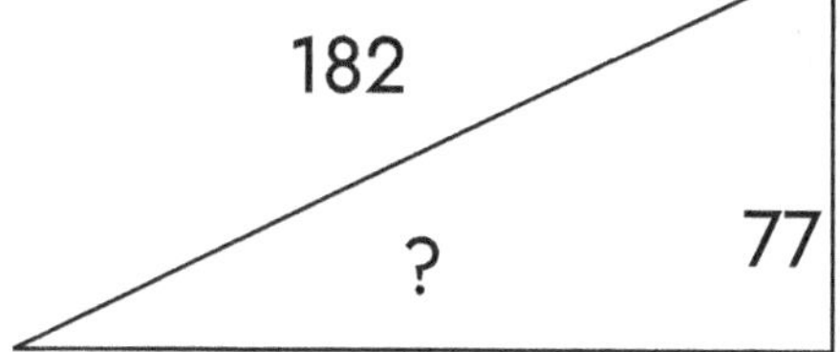

82.

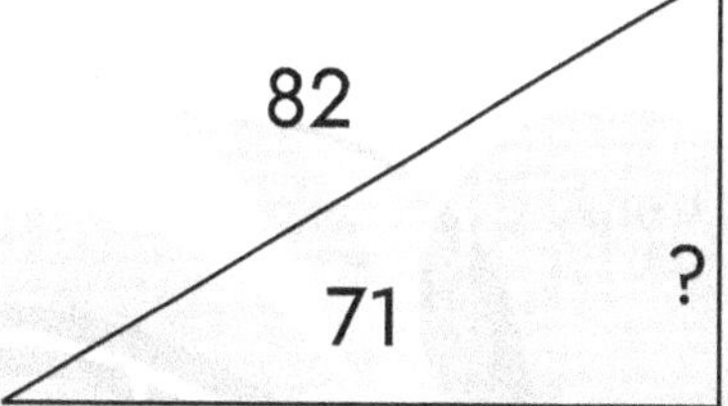

83.

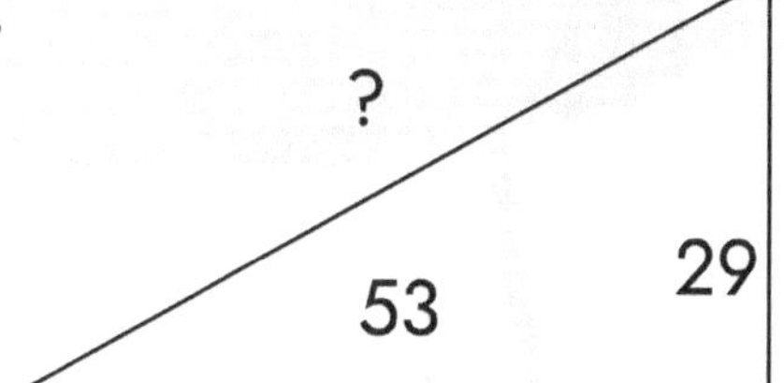

84.

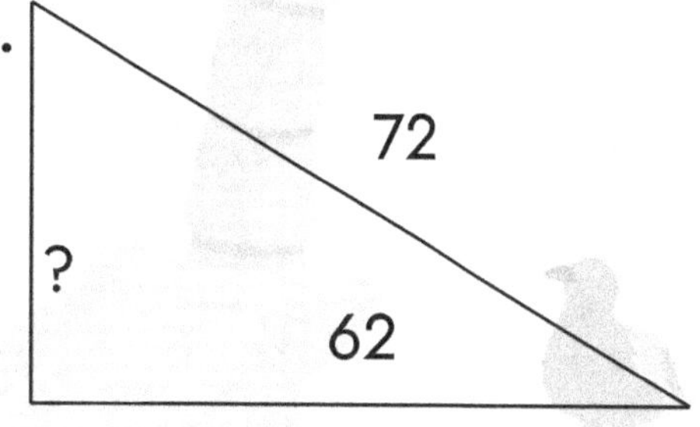

ANSWERS

Page 1:   Simplify Expressions

1. 21m	**2.** –19y + 22	**3.** 18m + 15	**4.** 16y – 2
5. –20x	**6.** –2z – 5	**7.** 32y + 119	**8.** 4m + 26
9. 18m	**10.** –15x	**11.** 22y	**12.** 5z + 10
13. –9z + 2	**14.** –24k – 7	**15.** –10x – 23	**16.** 9z + 12
17. 3m + 12	**18.** –7z + 14	**19.** 12x – 9	**20.** 23m
21. 10k – 1	**22.** –14k – 21	**23.** 21k	**24.** 96z – 292
25. 6x + 8	**26.** 37z + 11	**27.** 18m	**28.** –7x + 20
29. 9m	**30.** 13y + 27	**31.** 234m + 88	**32.** 12k – 9
33. 17x – 30	**34.** 16y + 22	**35.** –12m	**36.** 12m
37. 38y	**38.** 9m + 19	**39.** 23k + 20	**40.** 23z – 1
41. 156k + 102	**42.** 2k + 3	**43.** –2m + 18	**44.** 11z – 21
45. 8m – 25	**46.** 26k + 23	**47.** –7x	**48.** –27k + 26
49. 13k			

Page 11:   Solving Equations

1. 3   **2.** 48   **3.** 1   **4.** 2   **5.** 54   **6.** 18   **7.** 28   **8.** 1   **9.** 49   **10.** 45

Page 12:   Solving Equations

1. 1   **2.** 19   **3.** 8   **4.** 18   **5.** 18   **6.** 10   **7.** 19   **8.** 24   **9.** 8   **10.** 57

Page 13:   Solving Equations

1. 79   **2.** 15   **3.** 7   **4.** 12   **5.** 1   **6.** 45   **7.** 14   **8.** 5   **9.** 68   **10.** 57

Page 14:   **Solving Equations**

1. 60   **2.** 10   **3.** 14   **4.** 60   **5.** 112   **6.** 28   **7.** 12   **8.** 22   **9.** 12   **10.** 33

Page 15:   **Solving Equations**

1. 25   **2.** 16   **3.** 3   **4.** 3   **5.** 5   **6.** 3   **7.** 28   **8.** 7   **9.** 5   **10.** 6

Page 16:   **Equations (One Side)**

1. 13   **2.** 19   **3.** 10   **4.** 14   **5.** 9

6. 14   **7.** 6   **8.** 11   **9.** 3   **10.** 8

11. 2 or -3   **12.** 4   **13.** 6   **14.** 1   **15.** 8

16. 12   **17.** 1   **18.** 18   **19.** 8   **20.** 6

21. 6   **22.** 18   **23.** 18   **24.** 18   **25.** 20

26. 18   **27.** 15   **28.** 3 or -3   **29.** 14   **30.** 4

31. 15   **32.** 14 or -14   **33.** 1 or -1   **34.** 6   **35.** 16

36. 18   **37.** 12   **38.** 16   **39.** 16   **40.** 5 or -5

Page 26:   **Equations (Two Sides)**

1. k = 3   **2.** x = 6   **3.** z = 3   **4.** k = 1   **5.** k = 8   **6.** k = 6   **7.** m = 2

8. m = 6   **9.** x = 3   **10.** k = 8   **11.** x = 2   **12.** x = 3   **13.** y = 7   **14.** k = 8

15. z = 6   **16.** x = 6   **17.** x = 9   **18.** z = 8   **19.** z = 9   **20.** m = 8   **21.** x = 4

22. x = 9   **23.** x = 6   **24.** k = 9   **25.** k = 5   **26.** z = 2   **27.** x = 8   **28.** y = 5

29. z = 1   **30.** z = 3   **31.** k = 4   **32.** k = 3   **33.** y = 4   **34.** z = 9   **35.** z = 2

36. m = 7   **37.** x = 7   **38.** y = 7   **39.** k = 1   **40.** z = 7   **41.** x = 6   **42.** y = 2

43. m = 4   **44.** y = 5   **45.** z = 1   **46.** z = 8   **47.** z = 4   **48.** k = 5

Page 31:   Verbal Algebra Expressions

1. 2	**2.** 9	**3.** 16	**4.** 4	**5.** 10	**6.** 8
7. 14, 6	**8.** 2, 9, 10	**9.** 10	**10.** 9	**11.** 8	**12.** 6
13. 3, 5	**14.** 2	**15.** 4, 5, 6	**16.** 6	**17.** 72	**18.** 12
19. 1, 2, 3	**20.** 9, 19	**21.** 2	**22.** 5, 7	**23.** 12	**24.** 8, 16
25. 4	**26.** 3	**27.** 6, 24	**28.** 8, 12	**29.** 7	**30.** 1
31. 16	**32.** 7	**33.** 24			

Page 39: Standard Linear Equations

1. -2	**6.** 3	**11.** -5	**16.** -9	**21.** 2
2. 10	**7.** 6	**12.** 5	**17.** -2	**22.** -7
3. -9	**8.** -5	**13.** -4	**18.** -7	**23.** -3
4. 0	**9.** 2	**14.** 4	**19.** 4	**24.** 4
5. 3	**10.** -5	**15.** -2	**20.** 0	

Page 42: Find Slope from Two Points

1. 3	**5.** -4	**9.** 1	**13.** 5
2. -1	**6.** -6	**10.** -3	**14.** -6
3. 2	**7.** 9	**11.** 9	**15.** 5
4. -1	**8.** -1	**12.** 1	**16.** 5

Page 44: System of Equations

1. x = -0.39, y = 1.68

2. x = -3.0, y = 4.0

3. x = 6.0, y = -3.67

4. x = 0.5, y = 0.0

5. x = 0.53, y = 0.11

6. x = 2.57, y = -0.14

7. x = 1.5, y = 0.5

8. x = -0.5, y = 1.0

9. x = -0.21, y = 1.03

10. x = 1.31, y = -1.58

11. x = 1.47, y = -0.68

12. x = 1.2, y = -1.5

Page 48: Quadratic Equations

1. 3, -0.6
2. 2.4, -1
3. 2.288, -1.038
4. 3.75, -5
5. -0.477, 1.677
6. 1.5, -1.5
7. -1.248, 2.137

8. 1.477, -9.477
9. -1.632, -0.368
10. -1.64, 2.44
11. 1.677, -1.093
12. 1.243, -1.243
13. 7.5, -7
14. 2.853, -2.103

15. -0.603, 0.603
16. 2, -4.667
17. -1, 0.25
18. No real solution.
19. 3
20. -4, 2.667

Page 51: Distributing and Combining Terms

1. -2b - 4
2. -2 p
3. -12 - x
4. -14x + 7
5. 16 + 16b
6. -90b - 20

7. -3k - 14
8. -12 - 80n
9. -4x + 15
10. -26k + 50
11. 3b - 14
12. 19x + 70

13. $-32a - 16 - 12a^2$
14. $27n^2 + n$
15. $20v^2 + 60v + 35$
16. -4x - 10
17. 6 - 34n
18. -14b - 37

Page 54: Factoring with special cases

1. $8(x^2 + 4)$
2. $3v(9v^2 + 8)$
3. $2(8p + 1)$
4. $10x(4x + 3)$
5. $10a(b^2 + 4a^2)$
6. $7(xy - 3)$
7. $2x^2(7y^3 + 5x)$
8. $10(y^4 + 2x^3)$
9. $6(8k^3 + 5k + 10)$
10. $9m^3(9m^2 + 6m + 7)$

11. $2(2b^2 - 9b + 5)$
12. $5r(-2r^2 + 3r - 3)$
13. $7(-2 + 9mn + 10m^4)$
14. $9xy(5y + 2x - 5xy)$
15. $10y^3(3x^2 - 4y^2 + x)$
16. $3uv(-7u^2v + 7u^2 + 4)$
17. $(4r + 5)(4r - 5)$
18. $(4a + 1)(4a - 1)$
19. $(3v + 5)(3v - 5)$
20. $(3x + 2)(3x - 2)$

21. $(n + 4)2$
22. $(4x - 5)2$
23. $(2a - 1)2$
24. $(4x + 1)2$
25. $(x^2 + 2)2$
26. $(n^2 + 5)2$
27. $(5x^2 + 3)2$
28. $(4p^2 + 5)(4p^2 - 5)$

Page 58: Polynomials

1. $13n$
2. $4n^3 + 5n$
3. $-7b^3 + b$
4. $6x^4 + 7x$
5. $3x^3 + 5x^2 + x$
6. $-x^2 - 4x - 4$

7. $13p^4 + 3p^3 + 3$
8. $4x^2 + 14x - 4$
9. $-x^2 - 9$
10. $-7a^4 + a + 2$
11. $9n^2 - 5n - 10$
12. $-11m^3 + 15m + 4$

13. $28m^2 - 42mn + 14n^2$
14. $8a^2 - 42ab + 49b^2$
15. $6x^2 + 10xy - 24y^2$
16. $9m^2 - 9n^2$
17. $12x^3 + 11x^2y - 4xy^2 - 4y^3$
18. $15x^3 - x^2y - 48xy^2 + 28y^3$

19. $36u^3 + 6u^2v - 48uv^2 + 18v^3$
20. $49m^3 - 21m^2n + 58mn^2 - 16n^3$
21. $36u^4 + 66u^3v - 31uv^3 - 6v^4$

22. $25a^4 + 5a^3b + 54a^2b^2 + 16ab^3 + 32b^4$
23. $10x^4 + 18x^3y + 47x^2y^2 + 25xy^3 + 56y^4$
24. $12x^4 + 16x^3y + 49x^2y^2 + 34xy^3 + 24y^4$

Page 63:   Area and Perimeter

1. P=46 A=61

2. P=50 A=100

3. P=18 A=15.59

4. P=16 A=10.64

5. P=36 A=62.35

6. P=68 A=137

7. P=62 A=75

8. P=20 A=18.96

9. P=26 A=34

10. P=34 A=70

11. P=18 A=15.59

12. P=56 A=132

13. P=25 A=24.5

14. P=36 A=62.35

15. P=32 A=19

16. P=26 A=21.6

17. P=40 A=79

18. P=38 A=75

19. P=64 A=207

20. P=30 A=38

21. P=18 A=13.8

22. P=52 A=168

23. P=64 A=129

24. P=23 A=33

25. P=40 A=81

26. P=30 A=31

27. P=42 A=82.5

28. P=39 A=70.78

Page 70:   Volume and Surface Area

29. V=6 in^3 in^3 SA=23.2 in^2 in^2

30. V=65 ft^3 ft^3 SA=79 ft^2 ft^2

31. V=549.78 cm^3 cm^3 SA=377 cm^2 cm^2

32. V=13 ft^3 ft^3 SA=35 ft^2 ft^2

33. V=12 ft^3 ft^3 SA=32 ft^2 ft^2

34. V=48 ft^3 ft^3 SA=80 ft^2 ft^2

35. V=80 cm^3 cm^3 SA=112 cm^2 cm^2

36. V=62.83 in^3 in^3 SA=88 in^2 in^2

37. V=307.88 cm³ cm³ SA=253 cm² cm²

38. V=320 in³ in³ SA=288 in² in²

39. V=113 cm³ cm³ SA=113 cm² cm²

40. V=117 ft³ ft³ SA=152 ft² ft²

41. V=40 ft³ ft³ SA=76 ft² ft²

42. V=294 ft³ ft³ SA=266 ft² ft²

43. V=105 cm³ cm³ SA=158.6 cm² cm²

44. V=382 ft³ ft³ SA=254 ft² ft²

45. V=197.92 ft³ ft³ SA=188 ft² ft²

46. V=180 cm³ cm³ SA=230.8 cm² cm²

47. V=36 cm³ cm³ SA=66 cm² cm²

48. V=48 in³ in³ SA=80 in² in²

49. V=24 ft³ ft³ SA=55.0 ft² ft²

50. V=6 ft³ ft³ SA=23.2 ft² ft²

51. V=30 cm³ cm³ SA=68.0 cm² cm²

52. V=402.12 ft³ ft³ SA=302 ft² ft²

53. V=254.47 cm³ cm³ SA=226 cm² cm²

54. V=57 cm³ cm³ SA=91 cm² cm²

55. V=48 in³ in³ SA=80 in² in²

56. V=9.42 in³ in³ SA=25 in² in²

Page 77: Pythagorean Theorem

57. S=139.427   **58.** S=144.776   **59.** S=106.024   **60.** S=103.692

61. S=129.198 **62.** S=175.883 **63.** S=186.553 **64.** S=93.295

65. S=50.794 **66.** S=49.920 **67.** S=103.832 **68.** S=151.924

69. S=47.697 **70.** S=168.716 **71.** S=21.354 **72.** S=49.092

73. S=65.299 **74.** S=61.449 **75.** S=167.547 **76.** S=116.047

77. S=152.411 **78.** S=29.240 **79.** S=143.126 **80.** S=115.996

81. S=164.909 **82.** S=41.024 **83.** S=60.415 **84.** S=36.606